Editorial Director USA
Pierantonio Giacoppo
Chief Editor of Collection
Maurizio Vitta
Publishing Coordinator
Franca Rottola

Graphic Design
Paola Polastri

Editing
Martyn Anderson

Colour-separation
Litofilms Italia, Bergamo

Printing
Poligrafiche Bolis, Bergamo

First published February 1996

Library of Congress Catalog Card Number:
95-082142

ISBN 88-7838-013-x

Gensler

Gensler

The Architecture of Entertainment

Preface by
Ed Friedrichs
President, Gensler
Architecture,
Design and Planning
Worldwide

Text by
Anthony Iannacci

Contents

Building the Dream: Architecture for the Entertainment Industry

by Ed Friedrichs
President, Gensler
Architecture, Design and Planning Worldwide

In our globally competitive environment, instantaneous communication allows people worldwide to know immediately about the "best of the best"—in products, services, entertainment, and environments. At the cutting edge of the cultural revolution, which has raised performance expectations to unprecedented heights, the entertainment industry is setting the standard. By capitalizing on technological innovation, advances in electronic communications, and the revolution in retailing, the industry has made itself a pioneering model not only in its business strategies, but also in the creation of physical environments to house them.

The entertainment industry's leadership extends beyond innovative film-making to include marketing, merchandising, and delivering a variety of entertainment forms to a public eager for activity that can occupy its increased leisure time. Fueled by an extraordinary level of creative energy, the entertainment industry encompasses film studios, television and radio broadcasting companies, live-performance theaters, movie theaters, and multipurpose entertainment complexes, which synthesize entertainment, retail, and hospitality. The industry has much to teach the designer and the community at large, both about its methods and environments for nurturing the creative process, and about the public places it creates — theaters, shopping and entertainment centers, production facilities, and resorts. However much or little we individually frequent them, these places influence and shape the real world in which we live from day to day.

In a manner characteristic of post-industrial business in general, the entertainment industry has gone global and virtual, expanding its product into a mind-boggling array. Today, film, television, and live entertainment are the generators of multifaceted merchandising concepts that include videos, video games, toys, dolls, posters, T-shirts, CD-ROMS, electronic forums, themed restaurants, parks, stores, casinos, and more.

The physical environment plays a very important part for the contemporary entertainment industry, both at the source — film studio lots and television production facilities — and at its outlet — theaters and entertainment complexes. The studio lot is no longer just a factory comprised of sound-stages, actors' trailers, editing rooms, and offices serving one homogeneous and integrated company. Now a much-expanded complex, the studio lot contains, in addition to the traditional functional spaces, production studios and administrative buildings for transitory "virtual" production companies that occupy space on an as-needed basis, and marketing divisions and subsidiaries responsible for the merchandising related to a film. Gone almost entirely is the vertically integrated studio system.

The cinemas themselves, now driven by the pressure to maximize return on investment, deliver a range of products for a diverse community with expanded discretionary time and an appetite for an enhanced and diversified entertainment experience. Just as churches, schools, retail outlets and airports have gone from serving one purpose to being a forum for many activities — airports are also shopping centers, churches are community centers, schools teach children by day and adults by night, and retail centers offer themed attractions — so the movie theater is now the multiplex. It is a fourteen-hour a-day, seven-day-per-week hub of activity comprising, in addition to multiple screens, enhanced film venues such as ride simulators and 3-D IMAX theaters, bars, cafés, restaurants, video games and the highly successful entertainment company brand stores.

Today's entertainment industry leaders have many lessons to teach corporations about dealing with out-sourcing and downsizing while they create virtual enterprises to deliver new concept goods and services. Someone must give physical form to this fast-changing industry, and therein lies a prominent role for architects and designers, who, in addition to their technical training and skills, must understand what stimulates the creative process on which the industry is built.

Of all the aspects of the entertainment industry, one has remained unchanged: creativity. The making of a film, play, or television program still relies on the talents and vision of human beings. As the least tangible and most important component of entertainment, creativity needs to be cherished and nurtured. And in learning to incorporate this element in our work, our entertainment clients have been most instructive teachers.

The process of creating the entertainment product, like architecture, is by nature a collaborative enterprise. Consequently, studio lots and production facilities have evolved in the form of microcities or college campuses, complete with streets, cafés and plazas that foster the serendipitous interactions that stimulate creativity. Mel Brooks underscored the importance of this principle for me 20 years ago, when I was visiting the 20th Century Fox studios in preparation for a strategic planning project. His office, he said, was located in such a way that he could easily engage passers-by in casual conversation.

When the dialogue got interesting, it was easy to sit down in his office to develop the idea further. The possibility of such productive conversations hinged on his being near a busy path of travel that had many characteristics of a city street.

Another important lesson in creating a stimulating environment came to us from Mike Vance, who once worked for The Walt Disney Company. He described a young man who, many years before, had come up with the concept of "five-sensing." This clever young man's intuitive observation that people respond more strongly to an experience that stimulates several senses rather than only one has since been validated scientifically. Movies and themed attractions are conceived to appeal to multiple senses — sight, sound, touch, taste, and smell.

At Gensler we have focused on understanding this creative process and applying our findings to architecture. The setting that Brooks described, analogous to the streets and public plazas of charming villages or friendly neighborhoods, is easy to observe and analyze, but difficult to achieve at the scale of a single company. Yet such settings have exercised an enormous influence on our work. Our designs for studio lots and other facilities planning projects support creativity by incorporating town squares, coffee bars, and other urban tactics that bring people together and facilitate the exchange of ideas. Five-sensing has become an underlying principle in much of Gensler's work. It is borne out in working environments that, through their discriminating use of color, water features, tactile surfaces, proximity to views, even fragrant plants and other stimuli, challenge the mind as well as the senses.

The change in the entertainment industry has many implications for the physical environments where all of us work, for our social activities, and for culture in general. Planning a functional working environment is an important task for an architect. But designing such a place which produces an emotional response, while it supports the activities for which it is built, is where we deliver real value in our work.

Gensler's work for the entertainment industry has encompassed television and radio stations, theaters, production and post-production facilities, master planning of studio lots, themed entertainment parks, and cinema complexes. Among our entertainment clients are such companies as Sony, Warner Bros., Paramount, MCA, Home Box Office, The American Conservatory Theater, and The Walt Disney Company. We believe that our ability to keep pace with change and to constantly improve quality has enabled us to provide consistently challenging solutions for our clients in entertainment as well as for those in other industries. In collaboration with them we are able to deliver the most innovative solutions for today—such as the new Sony Theatres Lincoln Square complex, which takes showmanship a step forward—while building adaptability into our work, knowing that tomorrow's demands will continue to push the envelope further.

The principles of our entertainment design are also applicable to business and institutional environments at large, enabling them to be more productive and successful. We focus all our work on maximizing creativity and performance, while delivering technological innovation and creating a high quality, adaptable environment for our clients. Gensler's work in film, television, and entertainment is helping to define the industry — while the industry teaches us how to be inspired and creative architects for the other clients we serve.

Gensler: The Architecture of Entertainment

by Anthony Iannacci

Entertainment is an expanding notion in a constant state of flux and metamorphosis. It is something that is temporary and transient, and the permanent structures that support it have often attempted to contain some of the energy generated by this transience.

The Gensler architects, planners and designers have worked extensively in entertainment architecture. Included in their client list are entire film, television and radio studios as well as movie theaters, theaters, performing arts centers, entertainment complexes, and even amusement/theme parks. Their work in the field has gone from the traditional theater to the cutting-edge of retail entertainment. The Gensler teams provide a broad scope of services for their entertainment clients, moving well beyond the confines of architecture and interior design. Their work in the field is often deeply grounded in the construction of an image for each of their entertainment clients – and in transforming that all–important image into a real, functioning identity.

Having come from a background of working with corporate interior space, space in a constant state of change, the Gensler teams have invented a design service that is accustomed to relating and responding to change and impermanence. Within the turbulent entertainment industry adaptivity is a key issue. The Gensler team has carried what they have learned about change into their architecture and master-planning work for their entertainment clients. Since the late 1970s, Gensler has created architecture, interior design, and space planning specifically to serve the business and production needs of their entertainment clients, and the information they have absorbed from these experiences has become a useful tool for much of their more general architecture and design.

When considering the motion picture studios constructed in the 1920s and 1930s, one quickly realizes that these film production factories had very little to do with architecture. They were massed together as need and funds arose and, with some exceptions like the Thalberg Building, their interest to us today stems from the oddity of their unique building type or their place within movie-making history, and certainly not for their architectural merit. When the worldwide market for entertainment exploded at the start of the 1980s, it became clear to the new players that their structures were in severe need of renovation, modernization and expansion. The studios no longer rely solely on box-office sales to recoup the cost of making and marketing a film; motion picture distribution, television programming and syndication, theatrical exhibition, home video, operation of studio facilities, distribution of filmed entertainment worldwide, cable channels, and of course, video rentals and sales have been added to the list. With this influx of activity came an increase in competition and the need for more high-powered administrative and creative spaces within the studios.

With each of its studio clients, Gensler worked on the clarification of a corporate identity and culture through the development of a total scheme to pull the diverse segments of the studio together in a campus-like environment. As very little building was actually done on the studio lots between the 1930s and 1980s, the Gensler teams of architects, planners and designers played on those initial elements to create visually coherent, modern facilities. Today the Warner Bros., Inc. lot is characterized by the Spanish revival/Mediterranean style of some of its original buildings; at Paramount Pictures Corporation a sense of Spanish baroque continues through its new structures and common outdoor spaces; and at Sony Pictures Entertainment, Inc. the white art deco style of the landmark Thalberg Building dominates much of the lot.

As entertainment moves towards the twenty-first century, there is a growing cultural need to reassess that which has been accomplished. With many of their entertainment projects, the Gensler team has taken a look backward in the face of changing times in order to allow for this reassessment. The studios needed not only to show that they too had been through a process of evolution, but also to show that they are still part of this process. The studios are a place where change is a constant, and changing tides of ownership, the presence of changing production companies that come and go, and the relative short-term failure or success of their products have all called for a physical place that is capable of retaining memory while it encourages growth.

Works

Sony
Pictures Studios

When Sony Pictures Entertainment acquired the historic Culver City studio facility in 1990, it sought to consolidate its extensive operations under one roof. A major goal was to create a corporate headquarters that reflected both the richness of its own history and the renaissance of the legendary past of the property formerly owned by MGM.

Other than within specific technical areas of the studio, during the nearly two decades of shifts in ownership and management very little capital had been invested in the facilities on the 44.5-acre property in Culver City. A team of Gensler architects, planners, and designers worked intensively with Sony Pictures Entertainment to compile a list of over 100 widely diverse projects, which covered the entire site. This plan carefully guided the evolution of the rundown facility into the state-of-the-art studio campus that it now is.

This comprehensive plan, which was approved in 1993, included an addition of 1.8 million square feet of space, with the intention of establishing a primary residence for the company, restoring and revitalizing the entire Culver City studio facility, improving land use and creating a campus environment that would allow for open spaces and enhance the quality of the working environment. The fifteen-year plan addressed the company's short- and long-term goals, and included not only the replacement and consolidation of buildings along with the construction of new spaces, but also an intervention of some sort on each of the more than 100 buildings on the lot. By bringing all of their employees to the one Culver City location, Sony Picture's management projected that the transformation of the historic site into a full-service, state-of-the-art entertainment facility would contribute heavily to new economic activity in the region, significantly affecting the local economy.

The Gensler architects and designers were retained to create a dynamic environment for Sony Pictures that would enable the studio to attract the talent necessary to produce a very high quality product and to respond to the many recent technological changes in the entertainment industry. Instead of creating additional large, airplane-hangar-like types of spaces traditionally associated with film production, the new development had to provide more administrative and creative spaces capable of dealing with the new areas into which the industry's products are moving. These mandates led to the demolition of inadequate old buildings, the construction of new office buildings, the conversion of existing buildings into office space and post-production facilities, and the preservation of historic and landmark buildings already on the site. In addition to these projects, many of the structures were in disrepair, and the Gensler team orchestrated the preservation of the historic colonnade, as well as a renovation of the existing commissary, the complete refurbishment of ten screening rooms, and the total revitalization of the back-lot character of the studio, along with themed facades.

The basic infrastructure of the entire studio was also reorganized and upgraded. The Gensler architects designed a new restaurant facility, created public, landscaped spaces throughout the studio, worked on the routing of automobile and pedestrian traffic, designed site graphics, signs and studio directories the perimeter wall and gates and oversaw numerous renovations, facilities management projects, and utility upgrades.
Work started at the studio in 1990 and within the first three years of their collaboration one-half million square feet of office space had been remodeled, and Sony Pictures Entertainment was well on the road to creating an aggressively new, competitive image for itself while maintaining a strong connection to the studio's rich past.

Perhaps the most well known symbol of the studio property's grand past is the Thalberg Building, located just within the main entrance. The Thalberg Building was originally built by Louis B.

Mayer as the MGM headquarters in 1936, and it was given landmark status in 1992 because of its history and value to the community. The Gensler team was given the challenge of totally redesigning the building from the inside out to house the headquarters and corporate offices, along with six screening rooms on the basement level. Because of the building's historic designation, only minor changes were made to the exterior. The 1950s lobby was gutted, and terrazzo floors were designed and installed in a concentric art deco-inspired pattern. The walls were paneled in pomole wood, and a reception desk and a glass-and-steel screen were also designed in the deco style of the structure and accompanied by furniture from the 1930s. However, the Gensler team wanted to exhibit the wealth of history the studio carries in ways that went beyond the art deco styling. To do so, special showcases were designed along the walls of the lobby to feature the company's "Best Motion Picture" Academy Awards. Gensler designers also went through the archives to find historic movie posters and placed them throughout the public and private spaces. In addition to being furnished with state-of-the-art sound, film, and video equipment, each of the six private theaters, as designed by the Gensler team in the building's lower level, was differentiated by its unique architectural style, detail and color, from mauve-colored art nouveau to deep red neoclassical.

The original studio did not include what is now the Thalberg parking lot. This area was purchased by the studio in the 1950s, and Grant Avenue, running directly in front of the Thalberg Building, was a remnant of the time. The avenue served as the entry point for the east end of the studio, but did not make for a very impressive entrance. The Gensler team wanted to create an entry gate that would signal the presence of a major entertainment company. Inspired by some of the preexisting art deco details that were found in the Thalberg Building, the Gensler architects incorporated its lines in the design of the Madison Gate, establishing a style for the entire perimeter wall and providing an exciting portal to the studio. Lamps on the various gates replicate those on the Thalberg Building itself, and the fluting of the precast lamp bases and gate structures establishes a design motif that recurs at regular intervals in the perimeter wall.

A structure that originally sat outside of the Sony Pictures property and functioned as a mortuary was purchased by the studio and renovated to complement the Thalberg Building. The Gensler designers then incorporated this building into the decorative language they developed for the gate structures and the perimeter wall that surround the entire studio. The perimeter wall provided valuable security and privacy, and enhanced the street position of the Thalberg Building as it faces Culver City. The operations of studio security are housed in "Precinct No. 1," which also functions as a filmable facade. The Gensler architects designed the structure and the shell-and-scroll detail over the doorway was cast in fiberglass rather than iron. Many of the details found on the lot were designed by the Gensler architects and then produced as if they were movie sets, breaking down the distinctions between permanence and impermanence, high and low craft, and creating a bridge between the architect's world and the world that exists on the studio lot.

The historic colonnade was the studio's main entry from the time of its construction in 1917 until well into the 1940s when MGM removed the wrought iron gates at the portals and installed turnstiles for its employees. The turnstiles have since been removed, and the Gensler team restored the wrought iron gates and had exact replicas of the lanterns recast from the original detail drawings. The meticulous reconstruction of the colonnade included casting new Corinthian columns to replace the crumbling original plaster columns. The building to which the colonnade was attached was in such a bad state of seismic disrepair that Sony Pictures decided to tear it down and replace it with a new structure. New steel columns were concealed in square pilasters at the back of the colonnade to replace the support once offered by a substandard building. As current city codes do not allow for the same set-back, the new Poitier Building stands fifteen feet from the colonnade wall.

The new 31,000-square-foot Poitier Building, which hosts production offices, surrounds the original Poitier Building and is connected with it, internally and externally, through consistently streamlined art deco style and detailing. The 4,000-square-foot historic portion of the Poitier Building, which once housed the offices of Hollywood mogul Louis B. Mayer, was gutted and totally restored. Even the art deco style canopy above the entry doors was designed by the Gensler architects.

Through their work for Sony Pictures, the Gensler architects developed an entire discipline on the design of themed, filmable facades. A "back lot" neighborhood consisting of whole streets with period buildings and distinctive neighborhood flavors was designed for the studio. Virtually all the facades that Gensler designed for Sony Pictures are true facades, which are attached to or were made part of preexisting buildings on the lot. These facades have been embellished with substantially more architectural detail and signs than is typically found in back lots. In addition to being used in filming, these facades have been created to help restore the character and ambiance of the studio as a motion picture facility. Here fiction becomes history, and history is used to create a notion of the studio grounded in the success of its products. Creating a feeling of nostalgia within the studio also raises our awareness of the studio's technological innovations. All the moldings, friezes, brackets, cornices, and other architectural details on the facades appear to be constructed of a variety of materials, but in reality they are largely made from stucco and reinforced foam, which have been formed and cut by computer.

The original Capra Building was a windowless laboratory

building. The Gensler architects cut windows in the structure and surrounded it with a new steel structure from which they hung facades connoting a small-town courthouse. The new exterior, complete with landscaped park, transforms a bland, functional building into a back-lot setting where films can be made. The-six-and-one-half-foot separation between the facade and the face of the original building provides clearance for back lighting and a variety of camera angles. The building represents an example of adaptive reuse at the studio, as it now houses Sony Picture's High Definition Center and numerous producers' offices. It also represents the dichotomy that often exists here between facade and function - a relationship that runs through the entire studio and reflects the fictional spirit of movie-making.

The Gensler architects also orchestrated a total renovation and remodeling of the Cary Grant Theatre. This theater, the largest on the lot, was remodeled to accommodate a screening room capable of seating an audience of 350 as well as a state-of-the-art dubbing facility for work on feature films. The Gensler team also designed a new illuminated marquee in a streamlined, art deco style and a new lobby featuring a terrazzo floor that echoes the floral deco-inspired pattern found in both the marquee and the new doors to the auditorium.

As in the "back-lot" neighborhood, the Capra Building and much of the other new construction and renovation at the studio, the Gensler architects and designers relied on a particular mix of fiction and nostalgia to create an atmosphere of elegance and importance for the Commissary Building. For the Rita Hayworth Dining Room, a new steel and glass entry was designed for the formal 1930s-era dining room. Internally illuminated walls and honey-toned panels of faux leather were used to break up the interior volume, create private areas within the space, and conceal new seismic bracing. Adjacent to the Rita Hayworth Dining room is the Gower Cafe, which was designed with a simplicity of line and finish that reflects the quick gourmet fare served there.

A different sort of duality exists at the Studio Grill. This newly constructed building was designed by the Gensler team with a facade reminiscent of an American diner from the 1950s. The Gensler designers detailed the facade in brushed stainless steel, ceramic tile, and neon, while the interior is in a hi-tech, industrial style. Industrial finishes include galvanized metal columns topped with industrial light fixtures, a polished concrete floor and concrete booth surrounds, with accent walls created from sealed particle-board. The exposed ceiling within the space highlights both the building's red-painted steel beams and ochre-finished ductwork.

The team was faced with the difficult task of incorporating the TriStar Building, a relatively new, rather bland, aluminium-paneled structure drastically out of the context of the rest of the studio, into the total scheme. Here the Gensler architects created a new lobby space in a restrained art deco style to create a bridge between the historic buildings on the lot and the new architecture of the TriStar Building. A colorful art-deco styled mural was commissioned depicting the historic process of movie-making and large, art deco-inspired chandeliers along with a green marble and brushed stainless steel reception desk were designed by the Gensler team to bring notions of nostalgia and fantasy into a previously anonymous space. In addition to the TriStar corporate offices, the Gensler team designed four state-of-the-art screening rooms within the building. For the elevator banks, the team incorporated a fade-out of the art deco style. As one enters the depths of the building the art deco detailing becomes evermore restrained and is made to blend into the new architecture of the original TriStar Building.

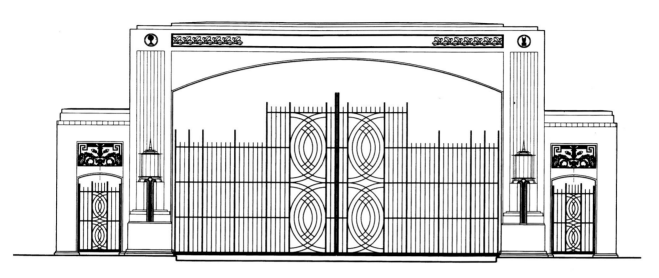

This drawing shows
how lamps and
decorative detail,
inspired by the historic
Thalberg Building,
were used for the
construction of the
Madison Gate,
the main entry
to Sony Pictures
Entertainment.

Master Plan Model,
Overall view.
A model of the master
plan, laser cut from
plastic, provided the
basis for early massing
studies of the program
needs to be met by
future studio
development.

Master Plan.
A later model of the
master plan shows the
buildings, current and
proposed, constructed
in greater design detail.
As realistic as it appears
in the light of the
noonday sun, the tallest
of these buildings is
only about 5 inches.

This drawing shows existing conditions at Sony Pictures Entertainment before work on the master plan was presented.

The color-coded drawing of the master plan breaks the 15-year project into phases and proposes the sequence that would ideally be followed in building it out.

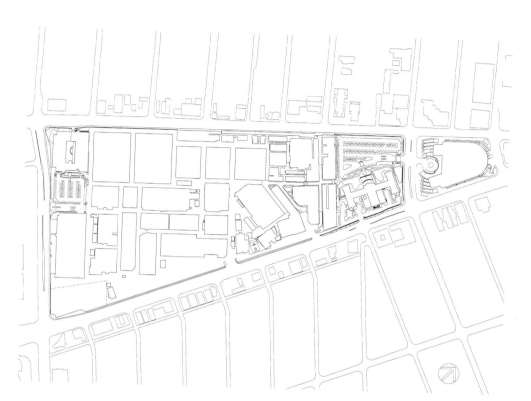

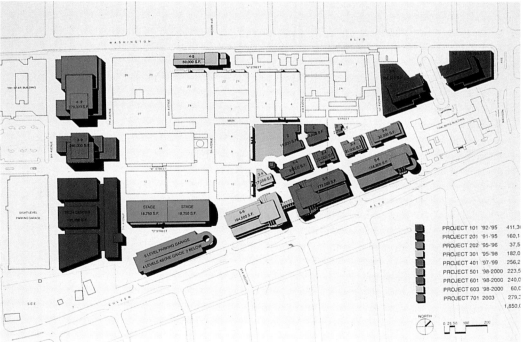

East Gate.
The luminous glow
of movie posters and
overhead clock create
an exciting entry into
the newly designed
interior of the studio lot.

Overland Gate.
The lamps, fluting, and wrought iron detail of the Madison Gate are reinterpreted for dual entry and exit portals at the Overland Gate. The Overland Gate is the major entry at the studio's west side.

Madison Gate, detail. Lamps on the gate replicate those on the Thalberg Building itself, and the fluting of the precast lamp base and gate structure establish the design motif that recurs at regular intervals in the perimeter wall.

Main Street.
The twilight glow of various signs and the pedestrian scale of the storefronts bring alive the memory of Main Streets in many American towns of 50 years ago. A giant billboard atop the studio's tallest stage can be seen from miles away.

Main Street, Creamery. In the quieter light of day, a view of Main Street features the Creamery, a favorite hangout for employees on the lot.

First & Main Street, looking west.
The Union National Bank Building on the corner faces the movie poster for "Guess Who's Coming to Dinner," starring Sidney Poitier, Spencer Tracy, and Katharine Hepburn.

First & Main Street, looking north.
The curved corner of the Commissary Building was detailed to showcase a movie mural. Sidewalks are flush to the cobblestone street paving to allow for smoother pedestrian flow.

Historic Colonnade.
The Colonnade, seen here in the amber light of dusk, stands as an architectural screen and symbol of the studio's commitment to preserving the best of its past.

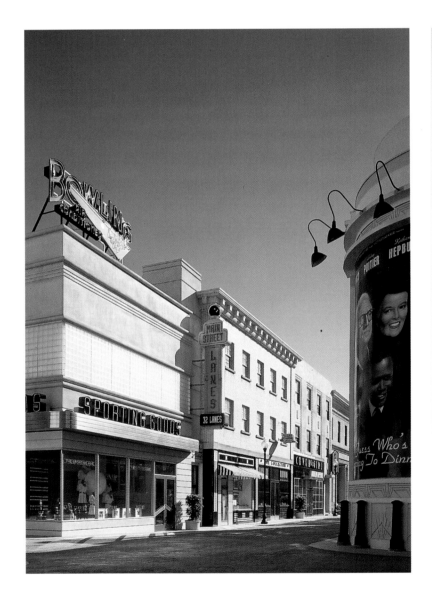

Thalberg Building,
Art Nouveau Screening
Room.
This screening room
is one of six private
theaters in the lower
level of the Thalberg
Building, each uniquely
identified by its
architectural style, detail
and color and equipped
with state-of-the-art
sound, film and video
equipment. This
showcase, which seats
approximately 50,
is distinguished by
its mauve-colored walls
and romantic plaster
details.

Thalberg Building, Neoclassical Screening Room.
This screening room features red silk paneling and, like all six of the screening rooms state-of-the-art sound, film, and video equipment.

Thalberg Building.
The historic Thalberg Building was dramatically redesigned from the inside out. Its exterior, listed on the National Register of Historic Places, remained untouched except for a coat of paint.

Studio Grill, Interior. Industrial finishes include a polished concrete floor and concrete booth surrounds, with accent walls created from sealed particle board. The exposed ceiling highlights both the building's red painted steel beams and ochre-finished duct-work.

Studio Grill, Entry. One of three new restaurants built at the studio, The Grill replicates the style of an American diner from the 1950's.

Studio Grill. The facade, detailed in brushed stainless steel, ceramic tile, and neon, is cool in the evening light.

Poitier Building,
entry doors.
The deco style canopy
above the entry doors
of the original Poitier
Building is an addition
by the Gensler
architects.

Poitier Building.
This new 31,000-
square-foot building
surrounds the original
Poitier Building and is
connected with it,
internally and
externally, through
consistent finish and
detailing. One of the
large production
companies under
contract to the studio is
housed here.

On preceding pages Capra Building.
The location of the Sony Pictures High Definition Center and numerous producers' offices in this formerly windowless laboratory building represents an example of adaptive reuse at the studio. The Gensler architects cut windows in the original Capra Building and surrounded it with a new steel structure where they hung facades connoting a small town courthouse. The new exterior, complete with landscaped park, transforms a bland, functional building into a back-lot setting where films can be made. Its six-and-one-half-foot separation from the face of the original building provides clearance for back-lighting and a variety of camera angles.

TriStar Building, Screening Room.
The Gensler architects designed four screening rooms for the TriStar Building, each seating approximately 100. State-of-the-art acoustics, sound, and projection make these rooms ideal for both viewing daily production and screening finished feature films. Stepped acoustical panels on the side walls are covered with lightweight, sound-porous fabric.

TriStar Building, elevator bank.
The elevator lobby features the same finish palette as the lobby—green marble, brushed stainless steel, and pear-wood. The floral deco pattern in panels above the elevator doors are repeated in other areas of the building.

At right
TriStar Building, lobby.
One of the most prominent features of the spacious lobby is a newly commissioned mural depicting the historic process of movie-making. Terrazzo floors echo the plaster color of the walls and ceiling. The large deco chandeliers were designed by the Gensler team to complement the style and scale of the space.

Above
Cary Grant Theatre,
Dubbing Console.
A state-of-the-art
dubbing console
in the foreground
ensures the continued
status of the Cary Grant
Theatre as a premier
dubbing facility.
Remodeled to
accommodate the
screening as well as the
dubbing of feature
films, the new
auditorium now seats
an audience of 350.

At right
Sony Pictures High
Definition Center
in the Capra Building
features both a facility
for processing high
definition audio and
video and a theater for
showcasing the finished
product. High definition
images are edited on
the console shown in
the foreground.

At right
Perimeter Wall detail
with Water Tower.
A deteriorating fence
has given way to the
handsome perimeter
wall that wraps the
Deco motifs of the
Madison Gate around
the 44.5 acre studio.
Studio identity occurs
on new billboards and
the seismically
upgraded water tower,
a traditional symbol of
all the California studios
from their early days
when they provided
their own water
supplies and fire
departments.

Rita Hayworth Dining Room.
This formal dining room honors one of the studio's most glamorous stars, Rita Hayworth. Black-and-white photographs of her contemporaries on the screen underscore the rich cinematic history of the studio.

Gower Cafe.
The pattern of the tile
floor provides the
signature pattern of the
space. The vertical black
drum at center conceals
a wood-burning oven.

Period Facade, detail of building graphics. Many styles and types of graphic design complement the facades of working buildings that double as backdrops for shooting.

Warner Bros.

In 1989, the Gensler architects and planners began working with Warner Bros., whose Burbank facility had grown since the late 1920s to include over 100 buildings, thirty sound stages, and eighteen permanent exterior sets. After relocation of all of the personnel from the old Lorimar studios to the Burbank studios, a newly combined total of 4,000 to 5,000 employees worked at this location. With this amount of real estate and density of population, the studio functions like a small independent city. The Warner Bros. lot operates its own fire and police departments, maintains its own phone lines, and operates an independent power plant capable of lighting a city of 36,000 people. An established entity of such magnitude, which continues to grow and change as it responds to the challenges of contemporary film production, requires new construction and the trasformation of existing buildings while it preserves its historic character and addresses environmental issues such as pedestrian traffic, parking, circulation, and regional transportation.

To this ongoing expansion and growth at the Burbank studio site, the Gensler architects and designers have contributed approximately 750,000 square feet of space. One of their first projects on the lot, which began in April of 1991, was a complete renovation of Warner's Commissary building, which dated from the 1930s. This work included the demolition and redesign of the historic Blue Room, renamed the Commissary, and the design of the studio cafeteria and 1,000 square feet of dining space. The plan for the structure called for a facade typical of a New York street to complement its neighbors on the Brownstone Street, which doubles as a shooting set. The Gensler architects were challenged again by the disjunction between facade and function. Here they were faced not simply with the contradictions inherent in a Spanish revival structure containing a high-end, high-tech office, as is the case at the Main Administration Building, but also with a distinctly

disjunctional relationship between two building parts.
The Gensler architects used this disjunction to advantage.
French doors frame the street entrances to both the
Commissary and the Cafeteria and fit into the facade.
The architects then created a sense of surprise and discovery
within the space by creating atmospheres that distinctly
differentiate themselves from the expectation established
by urban early twentieth-century facade.

For the light-filled Commissary, the Gensler team incorporated
smooth curving walls together with travertine floors
and eucalyptus burl to create a relaxing, soothing dining
atmosphere on two distinct stagelike levels. In a style
reminiscent of the art deco era, the Gensler team created a
curving two-step wood riser within the space that parallels the
swooping, sensuous curve of the wall and visually connects the
two tiers of the dining area. An intimate banquette was created
within the concave curve of the wall on the upper tier. With a
total capacity of about 200, all seating is finished in a lush
jungle-print tapestry. At the lower end of the space the
designers placed French doors that open onto
a large patio for outdoor dining, along with three private
dining rooms to accommodate small groups varying in number
from eight to twenty. On the reverse side of the curved wall is
the self-service cafeteria. Also designed to seat about 200, the
cafeteria includes a salad bar, grille, steam table, deli, and
central beverage island. Along the convex curve of the wall,
the Gensler team designed a rotating system for exhibitions.

A second renovation project was the two-story Feature
Production Building, perpendicular to the Main
Administration Building. The prime location of this structure,
actually five buildings constructed between 1926 and 1928
to house the studio tailor shop, wardrobe, and storage, made
it ideal as continuation space for the executive offices in the
nearby Main Administration Building. The Gensler team gutted

the interiors of the buildings and connected the series to create a single structure. Two new interior courtyards helped to reduce the massing and provided for more windowed offices. Two additional connecting structures were designed and built to unify the buildings. One of these houses conference rooms and the other is a two-story main lobby that creates the effect of a covered courtyard into the entire structure. The exterior of the newly created building was upgraded with a new roof, windows, and stucco facade.

Gensler began work on the Feature Production Building in April of 1991. The complete architectural renovation and interior design, which also included a seismic upgrade, new mechanical and electrical, and fire and life-safety systems, were completed within eleven months. Among other tenants, it now houses Warner's Company Store.

A design for the complete renovation and remodeling, with new interiors, of the Main Administration Building followed shortly. This building is located along a gracefully landscaped circular drive off Olive Avenue, among other two-story Spanish revival style structures, their heavily textured stucco exteriors and slightly-pitched terra cotta roofs reflecting both the classicism and the unassuming serenity of a California ranch. Warner Bros. retained Gensler to recreate the building as a unique classical and prestige-evoking Spanish revival/Mediterranean style executive headquarters for an organization that had evolved from a major motion picture studio into a worldwide communications corporation.

The exterior scope of the work taken on by the Gensler team included a new classical limestone facade and the creation of an important entry with the use of custom bronze doors and windows. The approach to this new entry entailed the design of one of the main studio entry gates, upgrading the paving materials, and extensive landscaping to create an intimate residential, campus-like feeling. The interior design and architecture maintained the languid grace of the Mediterranean style. The Gensler architects created an impressive two-story lobby with a graceful sculptural steel stair connecting the levels. The simplicity of the design and the quality of the craftsmanship create an atmosphere of understated elegance that is reflected throughout the interior, from the hand-crafted plaster walls and English sycamore veneers to the French limestone and walnut wood floors and satin nickel metal finishes. The renovation included not only a seismic upgrade, but also a total upgrade of the electrical, lighting, heating, ventilation and air-conditioning systems.

Warner Bros. required that the first phase renovation of the Main Administration Building, from initial drawings to move-in, be completed in no more than eight months. In order to meet this exacting schedule, the Gensler team orchestrated a major partnering effort that fostered among the entire team of architects, engineers, consultants, owner and contractor a sense of commitment to the project on all levels of production. During design development, Gensler initiated daily eight-to ten-hour work sessions with the extended team in order to implement working drawings and to meet the lead time required on the detailing and finishes. From start of demolition to move-in was 51 days. And the result was both an unforgettable collaborative experience and a memorable project. Construction of the second phase was completed six months later, in April 1993.

The following July, the Gensler architects and designers started work on perhaps the most architecturally complex structure on the Warner lot - the Warner Pavilion. This 30,000-square-foot building houses the Steven J. Ross Theater, the most advanced cinema to be found anywhere and an 8,000-square-foot museum for exhibiting the history of Warner Bros. The early twentieth-century theater facade, designed by Warner set designers to fit into the New York scene on Brownstone Street, inspired Gensler's architects and designers to continue the art deco styling within the lobby and theater as well. The 516-seat premiere theater sets new standards with state-of-the art acoustics and stadium seating to ensure every viewer an unparalleled theater experience. On the interior, the ceiling steps back in curved tiers that meet tall, slim vertical lights on the side walls. Bronze handrails that create strong horizontal lines bring a sense of art deco styling into the elegant modernity of the monochromatic space. In contrast to this, the facade facing the perimeter of the lot, which functions as the entrance to the Warner Museum, was constructed in a contemporary style that epitomizes public exhibition space.

The Gensler team designed the five-story Warner Triangle Building for a prominent corner across Olive Avenue from the Main Administration Building. Begun in 1992, the building design echoes the boundaries of the studio lot and simultaneously embraces the surrounding neighborhood. Its overall design reflects the prevalent Spanish revival/Mediterranean style of the original studio buildings, and its massing defines a large garden court on Olive Avenue, which visually and spatially connects the the Triangle Building with the front lawn and garden of the Administration Building just across the avenue. The building's monumental scale addresses the importance of the Olive Avenue thoroughfare by creating a gateway to the city of Burbank. The circular tile roof that tops its low tower reflects this key location, and the arched arcade creates an axis with Warner Boulevard, maintaining a visual and physical connection between the studio lot and the adjacent residential neighborhood. Even the freestanding three-sided billboard structure that once marked the location as the home of Warner Bros. and advertised its productions lives on as a key element in its architecture, reincarnated boldly as an enduring landmark for the surrounding neighborhood. The Gensler team's use of this ephemeral presence as a starting point for the entire construction, the logic of making something out of very little, of creating history from consequence, has provided the studio with a rich identity that is proud to rely on its past. It has enabled Warner Bros. to position itself historically and firmly within the city which has benefited so much from its presence.

Triangle Building.
The lobby of the
Triangle Building shows
that the strength and
grace which are its
hallmarks prevail in its
interior design as well
as in its architectural
structure.

On the preceding page
Triangle Building.
The building occupies
a prominent corner
across from the Main
Administration Building.
Its shape echoes the
boundaries of the
studio lot, while
its design reflects
the prevalent
Mediterranean style
found in many of the
original studio buildings.

Feature Production
Building, main lobby
entrance.
At the center of this
exterior view of the
Feature Production
Building is the new
lobby space that was
created to link two
existing buildings. Soft
textured stucco and the
tile roof complement
the Mediterranean
design.

Main Administration
Building, main lobby.
The quality and
craftsmanship of the
past are evident
throughout the interior,
from the custom steel
stair rail with hand-
rubbed finish to the
plaster walls and
limestone floors.
Upgrade of the electric,
lighting, and HVAC was
also a part of the
complete interior
renovation.

Feature Production
Building, main lobby.
The Gensler designers
achieved an intimate
residential scale
beneath the pitched
ceiling of the
two-story lobby interior
by the simple detailing
of a wrought iron
picket stair rail,
terra cotta pavers,
stucco walls,
and indirect lighting.

Main Administration
Building, main lobby
entrance.
In the new facade
design, limestone and
custom bronze doors
and windows
complement the stucco
to give the entrance
greater importance.
Lighted lanterns are a
nighttime studio
landmark.

Warner Pavilion, lobby.
The foyer of the Steve
Ross Theater
in the Warner Pavilion
is an elegantly balanced
anteroom that sets
a high level of
expectation for theater
goers as they prepare
to enter the Cinema
itself.

Warner Pavilion, Steve Ross Theater. The profile of the bronze handrail introduces a strong horizontal line to the art deco style of the theater. Curved lines of the stepped ceiling blend into the angle of the tall vertical lights on the side walls. State-of-the-art acoustics and stadium seating for 516 ensure an unparalleled theater experience.

At right
three private dining
rooms open off this
corridor in the
Commissary.
Their varying seating
capacities accommoda-
te small groups of
between
8 and 20.

Above
Employee Cafeteria.
The Employee Cafeteria
seats about 200. It
operates on the
scramble system, with
make-to-order salad
bar, grille, steam table,
deli, and central
beverage island.
Rotating exhibitions
are displayed above
the banquette along
the reverse curve
of the party wall
between the Cafeteria
and the Commissary.
Green upholstery of
contemporary design
is a cool touch in the
neutral color palette,
and faux skylights
introduce a sense
of light and airiness.

Commissary, main
dining room.
In this executive dining
room, a two-step wood
riser parallels the
swooping sensuous
curve of the wall,
linking the two tiers of
the dining area. An
intimate banquette is
tucked into the concave
curve of the wall on the
upper tier. All seating,
with a total capacity of
about 200, is finished
in tapestry with a lush
jungle print. An elegant
travertine floor, plaster
walls, and eucalyptus
burl paneling complete
the interior, all in a style
reminiscent of the Deco
era. French doors open
onto a large patio for
outdoor dining.

Paramount Pictures

Paramount Pictures engaged Gensler to create a design that would incorporate the existing studio lot with newly acquired property adjacent to it on the south side of Marathon Street. A blend of architectural and interior design, urban planning, and general programming resulted in 1992 in the construction of two new buildings, the Marathon Office Building and the Paramount Theater. The redesign, upgrade, and extension of the Marathon Paseo, a pedestrian walk which crosses the lot from east to west on the site of the old Marathon Street, unified the new development with the existing areas.

Here again, the client studio desired an architectural vocabulary that would serve to reinforce the historic identity of the studio lot. While incorporating state-of-the-art technology in the construction of the interiors, the Gensler team designed the new buildings in the Spanish baroque style of a number of existing, historically significant buildings on the lot, such as the Paramount Administration and Charles Bluhdorn buildings. Both the Marathon Office Building and the Paramount Theater were built to echo the belt courses, cornice moldings, brackets, and other details of these older buildings. The new construction was designed to pull together the existing and new parts of the studio and create a total campus-like environment that would simultaneously celebrate the studio's past and future. During the design and construction, the Gensler team relied on the extensive resources of Paramount Pictures to save funds that could be usefully applied elsewhere. The marquee of the Paramount Theater, for example, illustrates this approach. Here the Gensler team designed the marquee and then worked directly with Paramount's set builders to create it in fiberglass, avoiding the necessity of hiring an additional subcontractor to produce it in cast iron. With this sort of collaboration the boundaries between the fiction of the studio and the permanence usually attributed to architectural thinking were fused to arrive at an imaginative and cost-effective project.

The Bronson Gate, perhaps the most venerated and powerful icon on the lot, and one of the most memorable in Hollywood, was the film lot's main entrance in the days when the Marathon Paseo was a public street. Paramount wanted the Bronson Gate and what was once the street to become the figurative heart of the studio and the center points for the new development. The Gensler team created the circular Bronson Plaza to connect the Bronson Gate to the enriched Marathon Paseo. The brick-lined circular plaza with central fountain establishes a geometric form whose radii become the genesis of the new development. The 500-meter. Marathon Paseo intersects the plaza and connects one end of the studio with the other. Along this pedestrian route the Gensler team inserted small parks, plazas, stoops, and alcoves to create areas of activity and seclusion that greatly enhance the working environment.

The entry tower of the Marathon Office Building stands as a sentry at the east end of the Marathon Paseo, which crosses Bronson Plaza. The axis established by the pedestrian promenade proceeds directly into the entry tower and lobby of the building. The Gensler team needed to establish a vocabulary for the interior of the building that would respect the exterior style while meeting the varying needs of its users. The architects wanted visitors to sense a continuation of the Spanish baroque style in the public spaces, but not necessarily carry that style throughout the entire structure. The ground-floor lobby of the Marathon Office Building leads to a boardroom and screening room, which are Mediterranean in spirit, while the multitude of studio departments, as well as the studio's data center on the lower floors, are contemporary. On the floor that hosts the Paramount Pictures Ad Agency, for example, colorful sculptural columns and bold curved ceiling elements add rhythm and suggest spatial interplay with a thoroughly modern style. What is established here is a stylistic separation between facade and function, public and private. The Gensler team has fulfilled Paramount's request by creating a public image for the studio, in the facades and public spaces, that is grounded in the nostalgia of the studio's past. At the same time they have created the sort of interior space capable of propelling the studio toward its future. This dichotomy of style (past/present) and structure (facade/function) exists in fact, to some degree, in all of the Gensler work for the studios. To thoroughly understand the success of this work, we must constantly remind ourselves of what is produced there and understand that the studios themselves thrive on this dichotomy. Paramount Pictures, for example, is simultaneously *Star Trek, Forrest Gump,* and *Naked Gun 33 1/3: The Final Insult.*

Paramount Pictures further required a new state-of-the-art theater for film screening. Proceeding from this premise, the Gensler architects designed the space based on the acoustic and viewing requirements such a theater would ideally possess. Stadium seating was steeply raked in the rear of the theater for optimal viewing, and this necessitated special care in the height and configuration of the ceiling for acoustic purposes. The contoured and multiplanar ceiling "clouds," curved wood "light shields," and fabric "baffle walls" were all incorporated to help reflect, absorb, and adjust ambient and projected sound to specified levels. The site informed the process by which the interior of the theater was designed, and it produced an ovoid shaped building. The Gensler team decided to orient the narrow end toward Bronson Plaza and to allow the long sides of the building to radiate from that center. They placed the north wall parallel to the Marathon Paseo and allowed the south wall to rotate toward Melrose Avenue.

The exterior of the Paramount Theater reinforces the studio identity by taking its stylistic cue from the surrounding Spanish baroque style. The traditional, flowing script of the Paramount name over the Bronson Gate provided the inspiration for the design of the marquee that hangs over the entry. And, like the Marathon Office Building, the public foyer of the theater, which can accommodate 500 to 600 guests, is very obviously the interior of the building that is visible from the outside. The sinuous curves of the lobby, the grand flowing staircase, and the delicate wrought-iron staircase recall movie palaces from previous eras and add three-dimensional richness and elegance to the room, as well as offer graceful flow towards the screening room. However, once inside the theater, viewers can appreciate the contemporary design as well as the most advanced film projection technology capable of exhibiting film in five different formats.

The first Gensler project for Paramount Pictures, completed in 1979, was the Studio Commissary, an 18,000-square-foot dining facility with a seating capacity of 300. The original 1930s building, once the studio where the Lucille Ball – Desi Arnaz show was produced, consisted of two distinct wings that were connected by an open courtyard. Despite severe dilapidation, some of the art deco character of the original structure remained, and the Gensler team emphasized this quality in their design. The project called for three separate facilities: a cafeteria, a full-service restaurant, and an executive dining room. The space chosen to house the cafeteria was stripped back to its original trusses and a lofty, rustic atmosphere was created. The Gensler architects and designers gave the full-service restaurant and executive dining room a new interior shell with curving, dropped ceilings and corresponding raised terraces. French doors with transoms were incorporated to overlook the outdoor dining on the terrace, and the entire space, after years of use, maintains a fresh, modern spirit.

Marathon Paseo.
Viewed from a window
high in the Marathon
office Building,
Paramount's Paseo
stretches through the
heart of the studio
towards a golden
sunset.

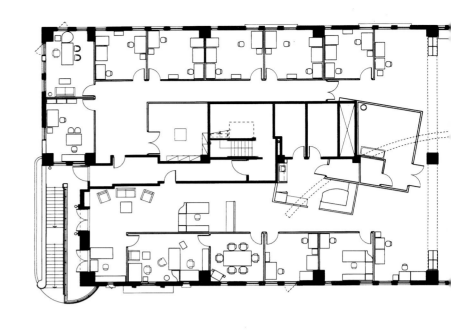

This plan shows
the relationship of
the Paramount Theater,
lower center, and
the Marathon Office
Building, right center,
to the circular Bronson
Plaza and the famous
Bronson Gate
on its north edge.

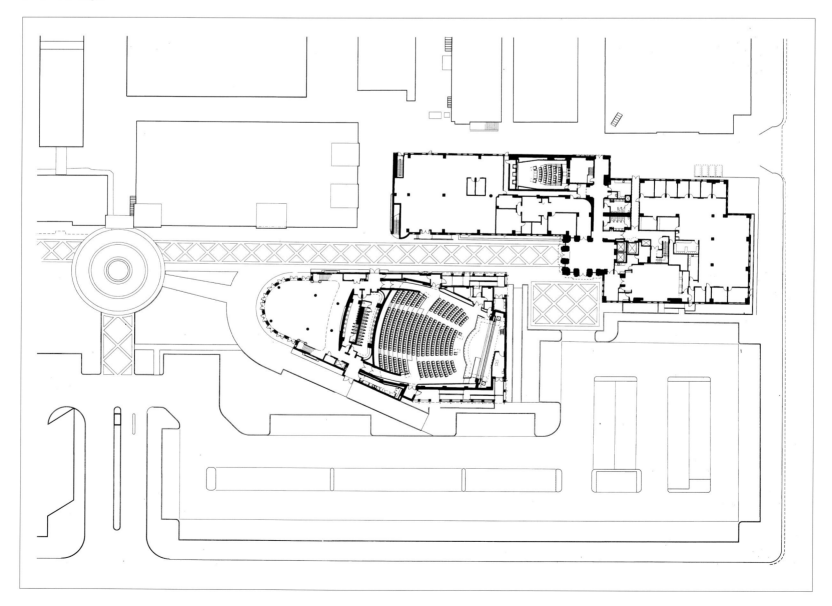

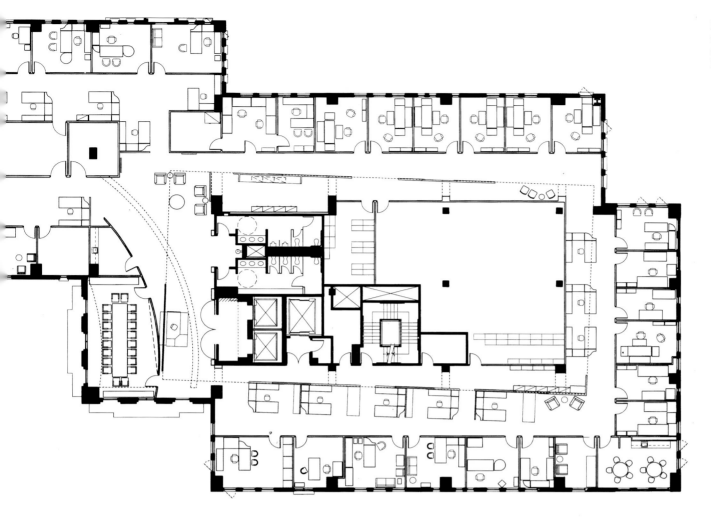

Plan of the Ad Agency on the 4th floor of the Marathon Office Building.

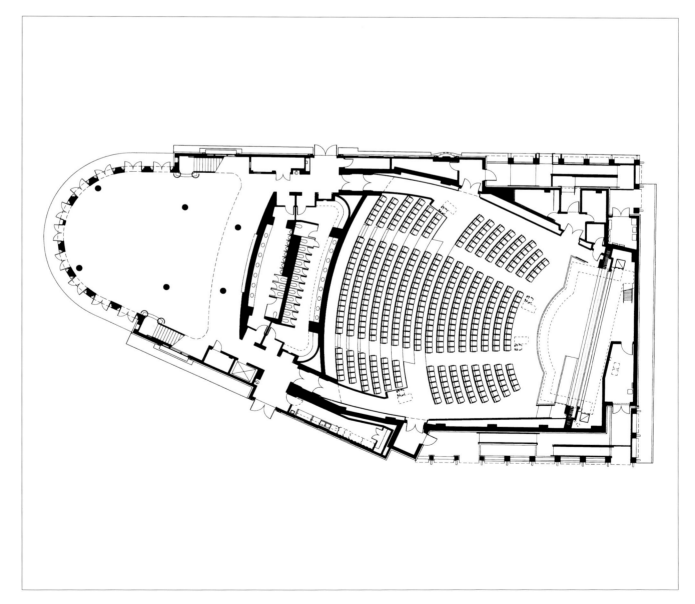

The Paramount Theater's side walls derive their placement from the extended radii of the Bronson Plaza and in turn determine the ovoid shape of the auditorium.

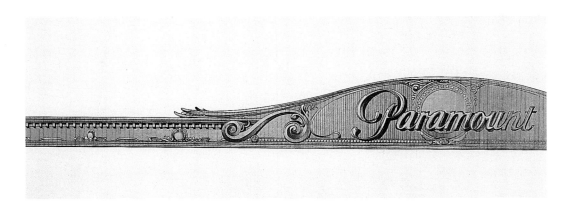

Paramount Theater, Marquee/Drawings.
The traditional flowing script of the Paramount name over the Bronson Gate provided the inspiration for this design.

Below
Paramount Theater Building.
The 21,000-square-foot theater reinforces studio identity by taking its stylistic cue from the prevailing Spanish baroque style.

At right
Bronson Gate.
The cornerstone of the new entry plaza is the Bronson Gate. An artifact from the days when Marathon was a public street along which cars passed, this gate was once the main entry to the studio lot and today is its most recognizable and venerated architectural icon.

Paramount Theater,
Lobby, mezzanine
railing.
Layered undulations of
line, heightened by
indirect lighting and
wrought iron, create
interesting visual planes
as seen from the lobby
mezzanine.

Paramount Theater,
Lobby dome.
The sinuous curves of
the lobby add three-
dimensional richness
and elegance to the
room, as well as offer
graceful flow towards
the screening room.

Paramount Theater,
Lobby, stair.
The delicate wrought
iron staircase,
embellished with brass
and stone accents,
reminds film-goers of
the grand flowing stairs
of movie palaces from
previous eras.

Paramount Theater,
Auditorium.
The 522-seat
Paramount Theater
recaptures the flavor
of movie-going in the
Golden Age of film
with plush seats
and state-of-the-art
technology. The theater
is equipped to project
film in five different
formats.

At right
Paramount Theater,
Auditorium.
A clear understanding
of relevant acoustical
requirements allows
for the creative and
aesthetic shaping
of the screening room.
Contoured and
multi-planar ceiling
"clouds," curved wood
"light shields," and
fabric "baffle walls"
help to reflect, absorb,
and adjust ambient
and projected sound
to specified levels.

Marathon Office
Building, Ad Agency,
Typical Floor Display Area.
In contrast with rich
linear wood panels,
suspended transparent
planes display graphic
material representing
the studio's creativity.

Marathon Office
Building, Typical Lobby.
A typical lobby in the
four-story Marathon
Office Building serves
one of the multitude
of studio departments
housed in the building.

Marathon Office Building, Ad Agency. Small areas are created to encourage impromptu discussion and interaction in a comfortable setting.

Marathon Office Building Ad Agency Corridor. Colorful sculptural columns add rhythm to transition spaces and suggest spatial interplay with the clerestories that admit natural light through adjacent offices.

Marathon Office Building, Ad Agency Reception. The bold curved ceiling element of the reception area welcomes guests and points the way further into the working environment.

Studio Commissary.
The first Gensler project for Paramount Pictures Corporation, completed in 1979, was the studio commissary, an existing 1930s building with two wings linked with an open courtyard. The cafeteria wing was stripped back to its original timbered trusses and has a lofty, rustic quality.

Executive Dining room. The full-service restaurant portion of the 1979 renovation has a new shell with lowered ceilings and raised floor areas. Curves, dropped ceilings and raised terraces play up the Art Moderne character of the space and eliminate the original "gymnasium" quality.

Commissary, Executive Dining.
The executive dining room features a series of French doors with transoms overlooking the terrace. The long glass table, which seats twelve, is surrounded by Brno chairs.

Bronson Plaza.
The figurative heart of the studio, the circular Bronson Plaza ties the Bronson Gate to the enriched Marathon Paseo and establishes the geometric form whose radii become the genesis to new development.

Babelsberg Studios

The history of Babelsberg Studios in Potsdam, Germany – what was until recently a part of East Germany – roughly parallels its Californian counterparts. Since 1912 the studio has produced significant films such as *Metropolis, Nosferatu* and *The Blue Angel;* its original stage building once hosted the likes of Marlene Dietrich. In recent decades, however, the studio has fallen behind the rapidly changing technology and consequently functions in aging and outdated support structures. The Gensler planners and architects were retained by Babelsberg Studios to create a master plan that would not only revitalize the historic film studio through a series of architectural and design interventions, but would also establish an integrated group of support facilities and place the studio within a new urban context for the twenty-first century.

Gensler's master plan for the forty-three-acre studio site is driven by the need to create a state-of-the-art production facility whose technological advantages and creative environment would attract major international talent. The overall master plan, which was the subject of an international design competition in which Gensler was not involved, is somewhat more ambitious and includes the development of a total of 100 acres. The Gensler plan calls for the creation of a *Medienstadt*, or Media City, around the studio, that would include a university for film and television studies, new office space for related industries, housing for employees of the studio as well as university students and office workers, a hotel, a cinema complex for premiere screenings and for public use, and additional retail, restaurant, and office space to service both studio and community needs. It also calls for a 175,000-square-foot entertainment/cultural center with museum facilities for exhibiting the history of cinema, conference facilities and interactive technological entertainment attractions as well as facilities for studio tours. The entertainment center, situated immediately to the south of the production facility, will become a pivotal public feature in the studio's new commercial district. The entertainment center will serve as the primary gateway for studio tours and as the main draw for activity in the commercial plaza. Here the Gensler team has expanded the notion of the studio from a private production facility to an embrace of the public with an entertainment sector capable of tapping into the history of the studio and simultaneously providing the newest advances in entertainment – from interactive virtual reality to motion simulators.

Gensler's master plan for the studio, to be executed in four phases over a five-year period, will revitalize this historic site with a series of interventions ranging from the renovation of existing structures to the replacement of others. The team of planners and architects evaluated existing buildings to determine which should be maintained as part of this ambitious program, emphasizing renovation and preservation of those with the greatest historic significance. The Gensler architects have designed several administrative support and production office buildings within the historic office-zone of the site. The plan also includes the creation of a campus-like environment with newly cobblestoned streets, a new entry gate, an executive park, and landscape elements with historic movie references to be integrated into the studio tour. Some of the new construction will maintain a relationship to the existing office buildings through the use of brick, stone, or concrete, but it will not attempt to copy their historic styles. Others, like the new production buildings, will host shooting facades like those the Gensler team created at Sony Pictures Studios. The new buildings include a 200,000-square-foot crafts facility, a 130,000-square-foot stage for serial television shows, and a 130,000-square-foot office building for production companies. The master plan further focuses on the improved flow of operations and the landscaping and development of land. A later phase of the plan will address internal circulation and operations issues and the commencement of construction of vital commercial support facilities.

Babelsberg Studios.
This Site Development
Plan shows the
proposed overall
massing and functional
blocking for this major
production studio.
The goal of the master
plan is to create a state-
of-the-art production
facility that will attract
major international
talent and result in
notable productions
for the worldwide
entertainment market.

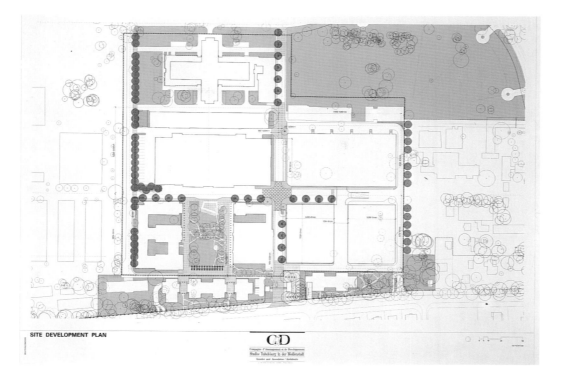

Babelsberg Studios.
Street Design Area A
shows suggested
site work. The proposed
plan includes newly
cobblestoned streets,
new entry gate,
an executive park and
landscape elements
with historic movie
references that are
to be integrated into
the studio tour.

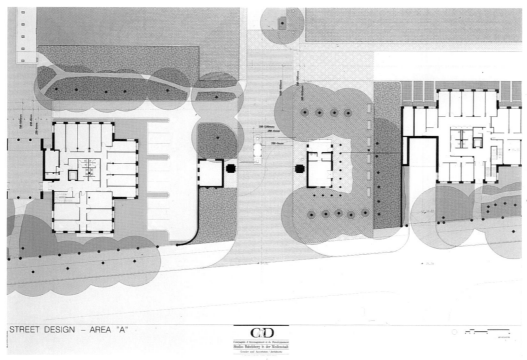

Babelsberg Studios.
Street Design Area B
shows the proposed
relationship of buildings
with the prominent
landscaped area and
new streetscape. Critical
objectives of the site
planning were to
maximize land
utilization, organize
work flow, establish
optimal phasing
opportunities and create
activity zones.

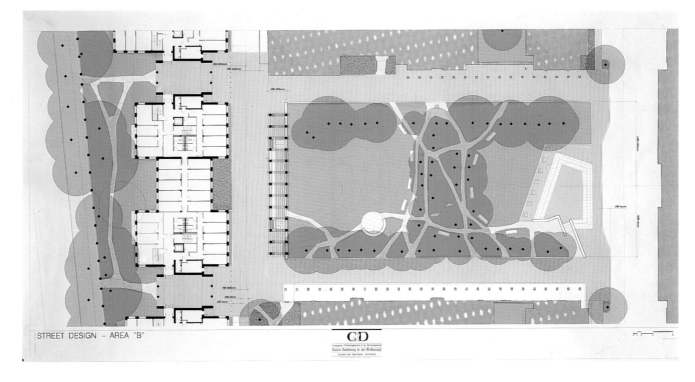

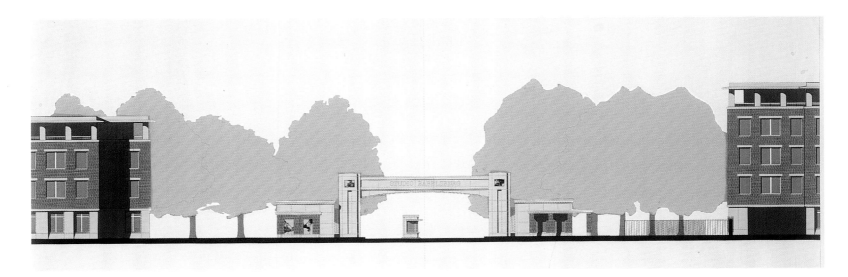

Babelsberg Studios. The Main Gate is symbolic of those years which previously brought the studio its greatest glory. It will serve as a landmark for workers and visitors and its image may be used to identify the studio throughout the world.

This rendering represents a view from campus park looking at the office building. Within this area of the site, the proposed office structures will have a relationship to existing historic office buildings. Massing and scale will relate without copying

historic styles. Again, brick and stone or concrete as exterior building materials are appropriate to reference the existing structures.

Babelsberg Studios.
A Television Production building is designed to specifically meet continuing daytime drama production requirements with automated light grids, dressing rooms, post-production facilities and support offices.

Babelsberg Studios.
A major new urban entertainment center is planned as a pivotal public feature in the studio's commercial support zone.
The entertainment center will be situated at the heart of the new commercial district immediately to the south of the production facility. It will act as the primary gateway for the studio tour and as the main draw for activity to the commercial plaza and will feature many attractions.

Studio
Plaza

In the early 1980s, prior to Columbia Pictures' eventual move to Culver City, the company retained Gensler for the consolidation of their operations in a single facility. The Gensler team designed the architecture and interiors for a 435,000-square-foot facility, completed in 1989, that served as the company's headquarters until they were acquired by Sony and relocated to Culver City in 1990. The structure was specifically designed to serve its own diverse entertainment needs, yet in a market characterized by an uncertain economy, volatile studio reconfigurations, and Burbank's Media District code restraints, the company also wanted a reasonable assurance of being able to lease the building, or portions of it, to other tenants. Generally, buildings do not adapt well; they are specifically designed, constructed and financed to meet the immediate needs of their occupants, not to foresee their position in the future. Columbia Pictures no longer occupies Studio Plaza, and the design has been tested by its successful re-lease.

The original challenge for the Gensler architects was to simultaneously satisfy the diverse requirements of the film company and construct a building that could be transformed into multitenant use. The building was designed from its conception to function autonomously, as one integrated unit with parking and landscaping. As all adjacent properties were designated for other uses, the Gensler architects located parking beneath the structure and reduced the building's footprint to create as high a density a building as possible within the site's thirteen-story limit, thereby gaining additional surface area for a heavily landscaped pedestrian plaza at the entrance to the building. The large, triangular, and multifaceted footprint of the building reflects its oddly shaped, triangular site. The total configuration of the structure was determined by the combination of this unusual site geometry, the need for underground parking, and a desire to create a building that would relate and respond to both The Burbank Studios and the surrounding residential community. The most imposing height of the building was placed towards the freeway, while on the south side the Gensler architects lowered the height towards the pedestrian approaches and plaza, and the residential community beyond.

The many-angled, saw-toothed design of the building provides twelve or fourteen corner offices per floor, and takes maximum advantage of natural light. By faceting the perimeter office areas, the architects created various opportunities for corner suites. This versatile plan satisfied the needs of the many company executives and producers, as it would individual tenants requiring smaller spaces. The building also features a cafeteria, executive dining rooms, screening rooms, and a 1,200-car, five-level underground parking garage, which is entered at three different points and takes advantage of natural light filtered down from a light-well in the elevator lobby. The principal entry, the cafeteria, and the executive dining terrace were designed to face the south side of the plaza for sun exposure and a view of the mountains. Three shades of French limestone, roughly cut for soft reflectivity, were incorporated into the facade and provided the structure with a warm color and accent stripes.

Once within the lobby, the Gensler team of architects and designers used limestone and anigre wood to extend the materials, color, and design of the exterior facade into the structure. The team also designed and incorporated bronze and glass showcases to display rotating exhibitions of costumes from Columbia Pictures' extensive collection and a display of the studio's Oscars and Emmys. On the remaining floors, the Gensler interior designers needed to create stimulating environments for each of the distinctly different groups occupying the building. The challenge was to maintain a standard for the building without inhibiting individual identity, creativity, or the flexibility required for a dynamic organization.

Each of the upper floors was dedicated to a different sector of the company – television, film, etc. – and each floor, while maintaining an overall design concept, was considered individually to allow for eventual reconfiguration. Most of the executive floors were planned with private offices along the perimeter windows and work-stations within the interior of the space. Both the television and film sectors consist of two-floor spaces and each incorporates an internal staircase. The two-level, semicircular employee cafeteria, which seats 300, is situated on the building's ground level, opposite the lobby. The stage-like upper level is connected to the lower level by ramps placed at either end. A semicircular row of columns echoes the shape of the space and supports a steel grid, which supports stage lights that serve to illuminate the space and establish an atmosphere of theatrics. The mahogany walls and cloud-dusted sky on the ceiling reinforce the drama of the environment. The executive dining room, with a full-service kitchen of its own, is located directly above the cafeteria and seats about 100. This space also includes two small private dining rooms for six and an outdoor dining terrace overlooking the plaza. The Gensler architects placed a fifty-seat screening room, equipped to project both television and film, directly adjacent to the executive dining room.

On the preceding page
Studio Plaza.
Designed to have 12 or
14 corner offices per
floor, the building also
features secretarial bays
on the return of certain
facets, so that each bay
has a window, letting in
more light and allowing
views of the mountains.

At right
Studio Plaza.
The crisscross reveals
how the structural
system is resolved,
where multi-level
underground parking
is on one grid and
the building itself
is on another, slightly
rotated. The interesting
pattern of beams
occurs above the well
that brings natural light
into the subterranean
parking levels.

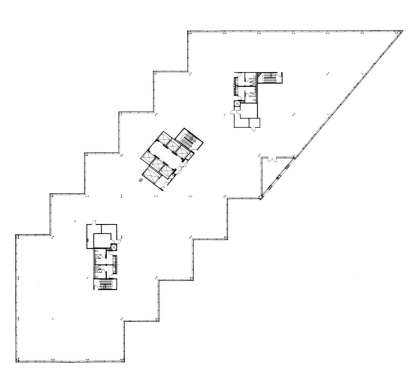

Studio Plaza.
The saw-toothed
footprint of Studio
Plaza reflects its oddly
shaped triangular site.
Central placement of
elevator banks, with
restrooms on both ends
of the building, work
for the convenience of
original tenants and
ease of possible
subdivision for smaller
tenants at some future
time.

At left
Studio Plaza.
The headquarters
building makes a grand
yet understated
contribution to the
Burbank skyline with its
multifaceted facade
clad in variegated
limestone all quarried
from a single location in
France.

Below
Studio Plaza.
Afternoon sun
dramatizes the colors of
the limestone in the
arcade and the
shadowed images of
the down-lights.

Studio Plaza.
Interconnecting Stairs
to Penthouse.
The Gensler architects
and designers pushed
this connecting stair
to the window wall
in its ascent to the
Penthouse to take
advantage of
panoramic views over
the studio lot, with a
nostalgic telescope on
the landing. The stairs,
with recessed lighting,
are finished in stainless
steel and mahogany.

Studio Plaza.
Stairs Connecting
Television Floors.
The whorl of this stair
links two floors in
the Television division.
A hand-sponged wall
finish complements
limestone floors
and ornamental bronze
handrail.

Studio Plaza.
Typical screening room.
Studio Plaza's three
screening rooms offer
comfortable viewing
of dailies as well
as finished films.
In this typical screening
room, acoustical side
walls conceal lighting
and speakers.

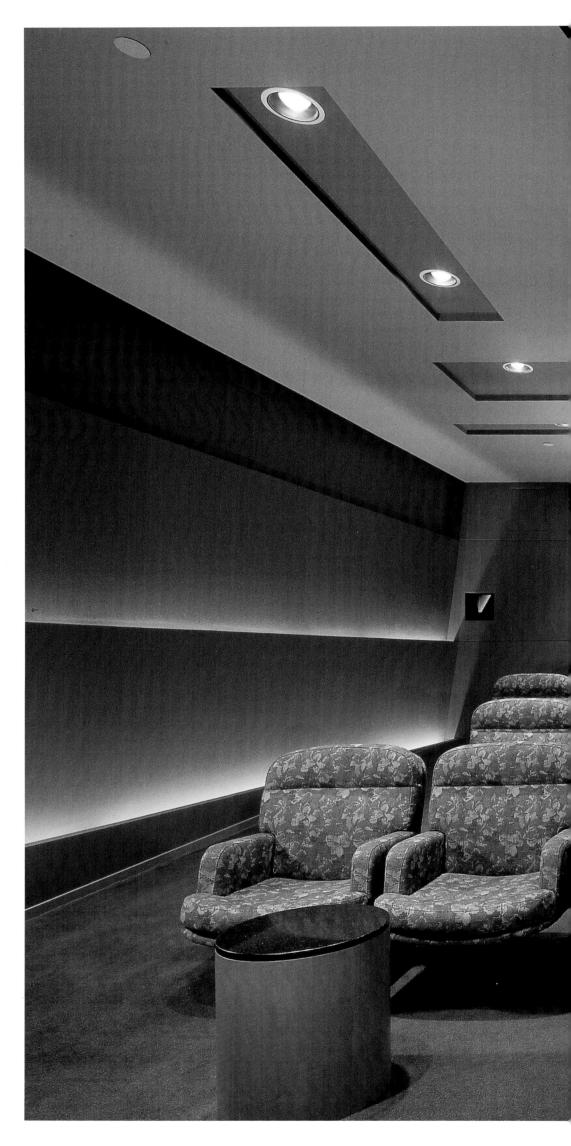

At left
Studio Plaza,
Television Executive
Suite.
A Chinese screen and
large bowls dictated the
need for expansive wall
surface and niches,
as well as the
characteristic style and
color of the Television
space.

Studio Plaza,
Television Executive
Suite.
Over-scaled custom
work-stations provide
maximum file storage
within the unit.
Lights on the corners
of each station provide
supplemental lighting
and an important level
of detail to the space.

Sony
Theatres
Lincoln Square

The National Association of Theater Owners in North Hollywood, California, reported that in 1994 American movie theaters sold nearly 1.3 billion tickets – the most tickets sold in thirty-five years. 1994 was also a record year in the industry for gross income, as movie theaters across the country grossed nearly $5.4 billion. An industry once fearful of cable television and home video's encroachment on theater attendence has found a new optimism. Today, energy is being directed towards providing viewers with an experience that is notably different from that which can be found at home.

New technologies are rapidly changing the movie-going experience, and at the same time the public is becoming more and more interested in choice. The flexibility to accept this change and the ability to offer a constantly varying selection have become the keys to movie theater success. The multiplex has gone from the badly hacked-up divisions of larger theaters to becoming the movie palace of our age. With screening rooms of various capacities, the multiplex can shift films from one room to another as attendance increases or gradually starts to drop off. Small screening rooms within a multiplex also provide theaters with the possibility of exhibiting what the industry has labeled "art" films that appeal to smaller audiences.

Sony Theatres retained Gensler to design its premier flagship theater complex in New York City at a site just a few blocks away from Lincoln Center at West 68th Street and Broadway. Started in August of 1992, the Gensler team of architects and designers were challenged here by the need to create an entertaining atmosphere, while including a 900-seat premiere auditorium, a 600-seat SONY·IMAX® Theatre at Sony Theatres Lincoln Square, four mid-sized 450-seat theaters and seven smaller 200 to 250-seat theaters in one functional environment.

The entire project for Sony Theatres Lincoln Square consists of a wide variety of seating and screen configurations, and the overall design celebrates the spirit of classic Hollywood while incorporating some of the most advanced technology. The Gensler team has provided visitors with a carnival of styles – Mayan temple arches, sphinxes, neoclassical festoons, pagodas, Spanish baroque wrought iron – and all of this is pulled together by a density of art deco detailing, star-encrusted terrazzo floors, swirling geometric patterned carpeting, a seventy-five-foot-high art deco-styled mural depicting some of Hollywood's great moments, and streamlined ticket, information and concession stands. For this project, the Gensler architects looked to the golden age of the movie palace for inspiration, and in looking backward they help reverse the human alienation often associated with the advance of technology in our dramatically changing times. The Gensler team directed their designs toward conjuring up a communal memory of what might have been the first cinema experiences of the average movie-goer's grandmother. The total environment they have created softens the impact between the emotions experienced in the theaters and the clash of the outside world of Manhattan. The Gensler formula works: the year Sony Theatres Lincoln Square opened, it became the highest-grossing movie theater complex in the United States.

The Gensler team created the atrium, lobbies and concession halls on a grand scale. Upon entering, movie-goers walk over whimsical star-encrusted terrazzo floors, acquire their tickets, and ride the longest freestanding escalator in New York, rising four stories, through the atrium lobby and past the seventy-five-foot-high mural of Hollywood legends to one side and a glass wall that offers great views of New York's west side to the other. The glass wall also exposes the interior, turning it into lively street theater that attracts outside attention.

Two grand portals line the first landing. To the right is the entry to the 900-seat "Loews" premiere theater, which features a classic, stadium-raked balcony and a proscenium arch that graces an oversized sixty-five-by-thirty-foot curved screen. Ornate appointments decorate the house, and intricately hand-carved details crown the gilded columns positioned throughout the space. To the left is the entrance to the concession hall and eight auditoriums. For this entrance, the Gensler designers created a replica of the stately stone gates that mark the entrance to Sony Pictures Entertainment, main production lot in Burbank, California.

Once inside the hall, one is confronted by a series of elaborate decorations in a theme-park style that pay homage to famous Loews movie palaces of the 1920s and 1930s. The Loews Theatres chain was acquired by Sony through its purchase of Columbia Pictures in 1989. The Gensler team framed the entrance to each theater with a miniature, stylized replica of such venerable marquees as the Valencia, The Kings, The State, The Olympia, The Capitol, The Paradise, The Avalon and The Majestic. At the far end of this hall a grove of tall gilded palm trees has been designed to support video monitors weighing a total of three tons that announce current or future movies. The concession counters in this area were designed by the Gensler team in an art deco style that reflects the spirit of the overall design.

An additional escalator carries movie-goers to the three-dimensional marvels of the 600-seat the SONY•IMAX® Theatre at Sony Theatres Lincoln Square, whose eighty-by-hundred-foot screen is among the largest now in use, one of the reasons why the theater has become a tourist attraction in its own right. Once within the theater, viewers receive lightweight 3-D headsets equipped with liquid-crystal lenses. These headsets represent the latest advancement in this visual medium and are unlike anything ever seen in a movie theater in the United States. In addition to the total immersion of the three-dimensional visual experience, for films incorporating 3-D sound, the theater is the first in the world to have the capacity to create multidimensional, dynamic audio through the use of the IMAX® Personal Sound Environment (IMAX® PSE™). By incorporating directional speakers into the headsets, IMAX® Personal Sound Environment (IMAX® PSE™) has the capacity to expand the theater's six-channel digital sound system, creating an experience unlike anything coming out of cable television or home video.

The Gensler architects and designers have created for Sony Theatres Lincoln Square an environment that allows people to entertain their fantasies, and the presence of this environment has had an effect on the immediate surroundings. Since pedestrians attracted to the theaters are already thinking of leisure time, the area quickly began to attract music, book, and sporting goods shops, and has become a spontaneous model for urban entertainment complexes offering a merchandise mix of books, music, movies, and all sorts of commodities related to leisure time.

On the preceding page Sony Theatres Lincoln Square, Exterior, from Broadway.
At night, the main lobby becomes a theatrical shadowbox silhouetted by the building's skin and framing the giant mural. Theater-goers become part of the theatrical composition as they ride crisscrossing escalators in the lobby space.

Entrances to individual theaters (these pages and following) announce their names, derived from some of the most famous of the old Loews Theaters. Inspiration for their design motifs derives from the same exotic fantasy evoked by movie houses of bygone years.

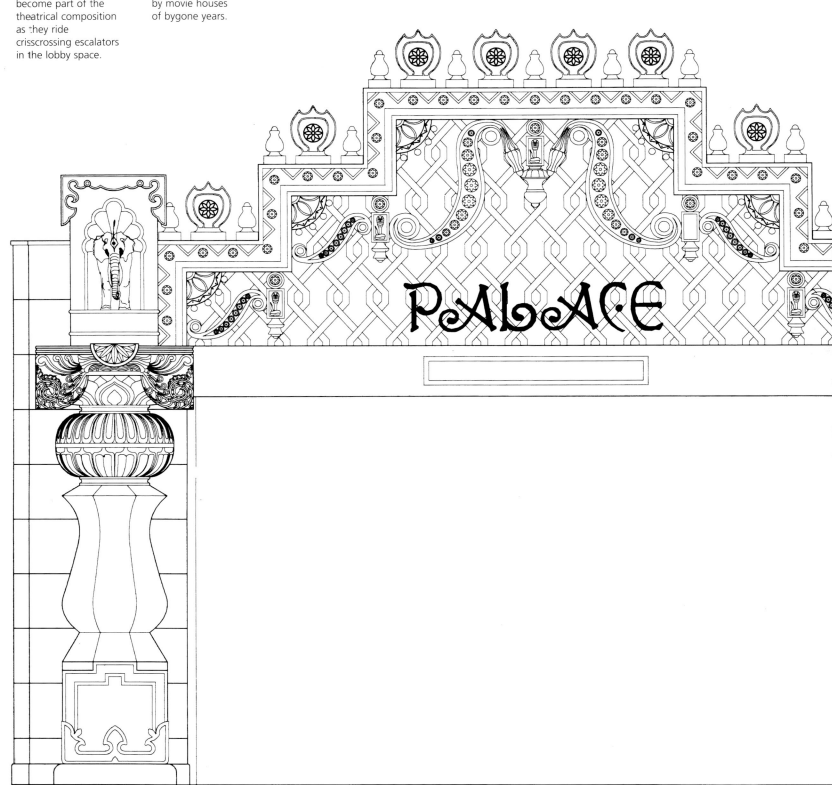

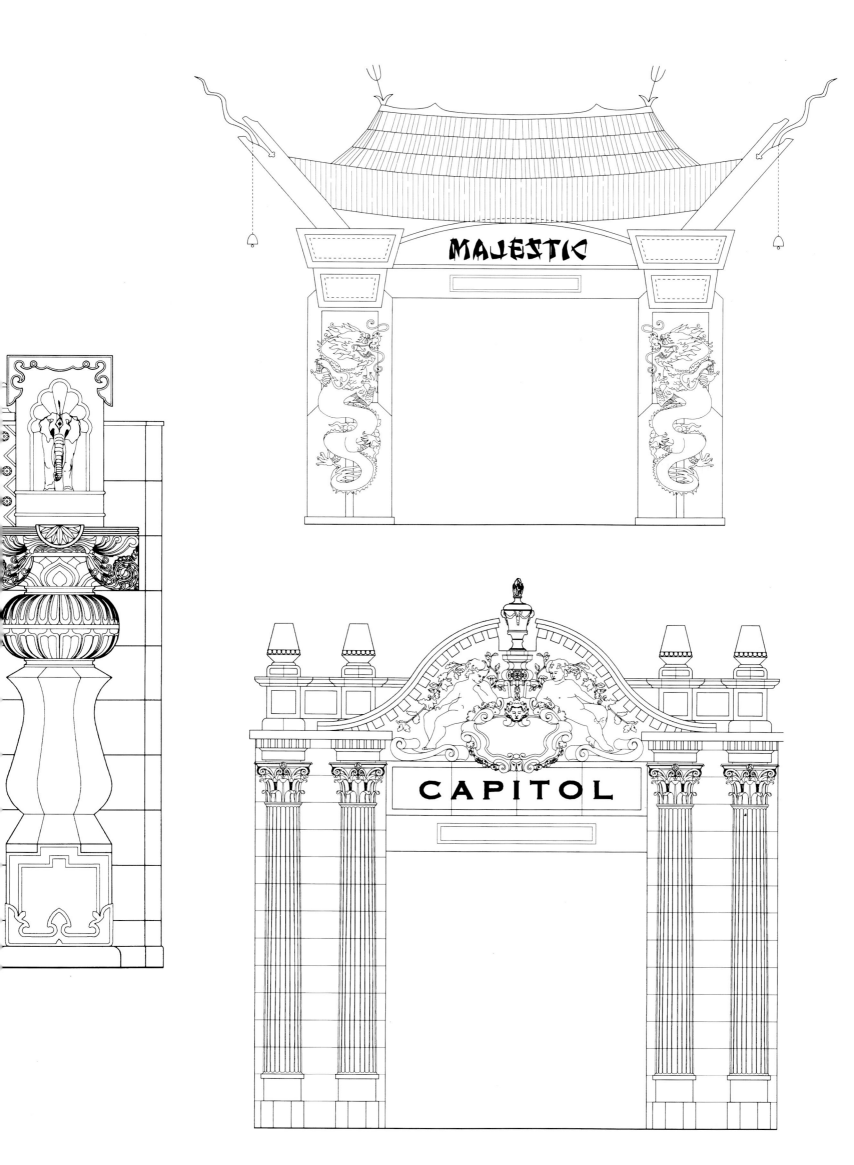

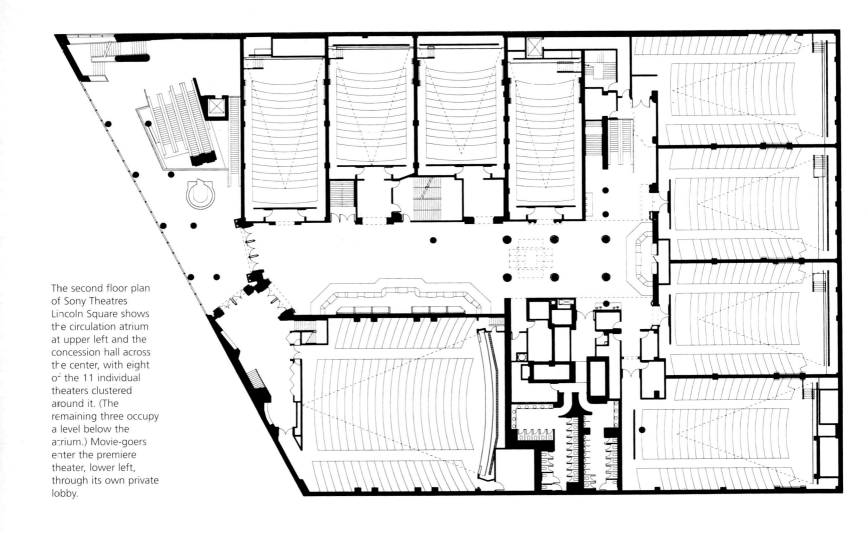

The second floor plan of Sony Theatres Lincoln Square shows the circulation atrium at upper left and the concession hall across the center, with eight of the 11 individual theaters clustered around it. (The remaining three occupy a level below the atrium.) Movie-goers enter the premiere theater, lower left, through its own private lobby.

Sony Theatres Lincoln Square, Lobby Mural, Close-up.
The mural is 75 feet high and half a city block long. It celebrates the history of motion picture palaces and the specific history of Loews Theatres. The mural was conceived by the Gensler team of designers and architects and executed by Evergreen Painting Studios of New York.

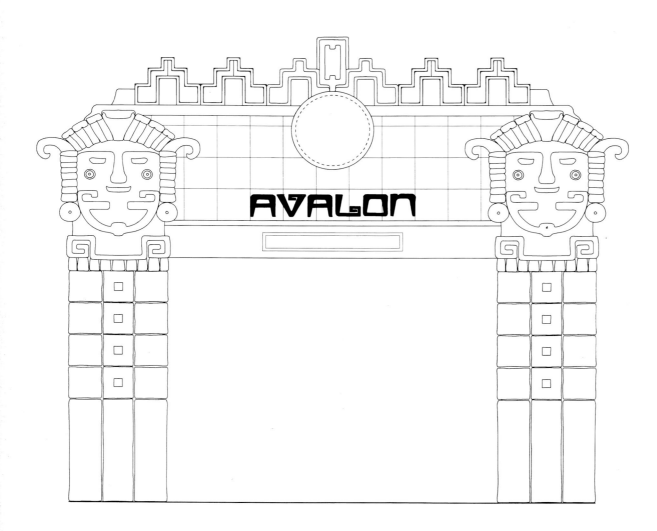

Sony Theatres Lincoln
Square, Lobby, Box
Office.
Sony Theatres' ticket
lobby features black-
and-white terrazzo
floors with an inset of
bronze stars. The ticket
counter, or box office,
houses eight sales
stations in a structure
that recalls a theatrical
style from the Thirties.

Sony Theatres Lincoln
Square, Lobby, Entry
to Concession Hall.
The entry to the main
Concession Hall is
framed by a replica
of the ceremonial entry
gates to Sony Pictures
Studios in Hollywood.
A large information
desk in the foreground
is detailed in black
granite and brushed
stainless steel.

Sony Theatres Lincoln Square, Palm Grove in main Concession Hall. The theater complex offers four concession areas. Shown here is a grove of black-and-gold palm trees flanking tandem banks of Sony's high resolution monitors. Concession counters are detailed in black granite, stainless steel and brass, and feature monitors that animate images of both food and beverages.

Sony Theatres Lincoln
Square.
An eight-foot-diameter
clock is featured in the
lower-level concession
lobby, complete with
Harold Lloyd hanging
from its face. Thematic
gilded portal can be
seen in the foreground.

Paradise Theatre entrance, with Timeline Column, left.
Each individual theater in the complex is named for a famous Loews' movie palace from the past. Seen here is the entry to the Paradise Theatre. An Egyptian theme is introduced in the highly detailed entry portal and carried in lesser form to the auditorium. The red column in view at the left displays a timeline for the history of motion pictures.

Sony Theatres Lincoln Square.
The framed entry to the Jersey Theatre features the theater's crest and a gilded dragon.

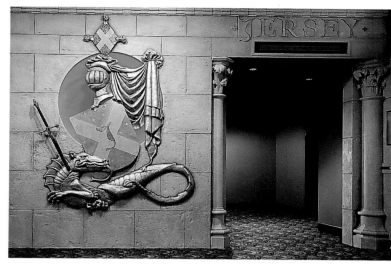

Sony Theatres Lincoln Square, Majestic Theatre entrance.
The entry portal to the Majestic Theatre is a confection of Chinese motifs finished in red lacquer and gold leaf. Adjacent to each theater entry is a bronze plaque that gives a brief history of the original namesake theater.

At left
Sony Theatres Lincoln
Square, the
SONY•IMAX® Theatre
at Sony Theatres
Lincoln Square, interior,
facing screen.
The screen of the
SONY•IMAX® Theatre
at Sony Theatres
Lincoln Square is 80
feet high. A pre-show
of light and music
precedes each feature.
Infrared trasmittors
along side walls in the
theater send signals to
3-D headsets worn by
theater-goers to create
the state-of-the-art 3-D
imagery which they
perceive on the screen.

Sony Theatres Lincoln
Square, interior of
Majestic Theatre.
The interior of the
Majestic Theatre is
typical of the mid-size
and smaller
auditoriums. Walls and
seats are upholstered in
charcoal fabric to
highlight the three-
dimensional panels that
carry the theater's
signature theme. In the
case of the Majestic,
the theme is Chinese.

Sony Theatres Lincoln Square, King's Theatre, floor tile design.
The entry floor at the King's Theatre is a mosaic of glass and ceramic tiles.

Sony Theatres Lincoln Square, lobby.
Directional signage throughout the theater complex is deco in style, combining brushed stainless steel with black.

At right
Sony Theatres Lincoln Square, Loews Premiere Theatre.
The premier theater in the complex bears the name Loews. With seating on two levels for almost 900 movie-goers, it honors Loews' famous Seventy-Second Street Theatre, which was designed in lavish Hindu style. Gensler designed this auditorium to reference the original, with gilded elephants and cobras flanking the proscenium arch and key details along the sides and balcony. The auditorium is richly finished in red and gold appropriate to its role as showcase for premiere films. The Gensler architects detailed the acoustical ceiling with pyramidal foam shapes upholstered in gold fabric.

Battersea
Power Station

The key to the success of the Sony Theatres Lincoln Square multiplex lies not only in the choices the multiplex offers, but above all in the entertainment value offered by the architecture Gensler's designers have created – by the place itself. For the proposed Battersea Power Station entertainment complex, this notion is carried further to become a total urban entertainment center that is equal parts shopping mall, world's fair, multiplex, sports arena, and theater district, all woven from a fabric of the highest technology available. The former Battersea Power Station, located on the south bank of the Thames River in London, is to become the centerpiece of a significant development for the area which, in addition to a premier interactive entertainment venue, will also include a Conference and Convention Center, an 8,000-seat arena and residential components, along with offices and hotel rooms.

According to the Gensler plan, the Battersea Power Station will include sports attractions, themed retail stores, specialty retail stores, restaurants, and nightclubs, along with special format theaters, museum and gallery spaces, interactive arcades and motion simulators, and a child play center. The plan also calls for extensive public transportation improvements that will have the capacity to carry more than 10,000 visitors per hour into the Power Station: a rail line from Victoria Station will arrive at a new Battersea Power Station stop; ferries will carry visitors up and down the river; and existing bus services, on the Battersea Park and Queenstown lines will be enhanced.

The transformed Battersea Power Station will be entered from either end of what was once the elaborate art deco turbine hall. Once restored, this area will become a Festival Hall, which will be filled with retail, food and museum or exhibition components. Visitors will move from this Festival Hall through the colonnade and into the main event space, a 150-foot-high totally controlled theatrical environment. The enormous size of these interior spaces is in itself unprecedented in the United Kingdom. A simulated "sky" above the main event space will allow for lighting transitions from daytime to nighttime. At the base of the stadium-like space, a "Roman" amphitheater, with terraced seating for an audience of up to several thousand spectators, will offer possibilities for staged athletic and performance events. Above the colonnade, the Gensler plan calls for a 100-foot-tall mural composed of layers of interactive video, moving and still images capable of transforming the space at regular intervals. The Gensler team has planned for escalators of extraordinary length to take visitors through the entire environment of the event space and up through the "sky" to the upper levels, where themed retail stores, amusement arcade, theater-like motion simulators, nightclubs, theaters and a winter garden will be featured. Once above the "sky" the plan calls for the creation of an environment where natural light and vegetation will become the focus, as opposed to the controlled theatrical environments that exist below.

The four tall white stacks on the historically preserved shell of the old Battersea Power Station comprise a unique landmark on the south bank of the Thames River. Light and large-scale moving projections will be used on the facade instead of traditional architectural intervention to transform the exterior into a kinetic beacon glowing on the horizon and signaling entertainment. The strong qualities of scale, historic prominence, and past usage of the Power Station have provided a framework for the Gensler team in making possible a kind of "otherworldliness" through a combination of wonderment and contrast.

Battersea Power Station.
Aerial view of existing site. The four tall white stacks on the historically preserved shell of the old Battersea Power Station comprise a unique landmark on the south bank of the Thames River as it passes through London, much as the raised flag above Shakespeare's Globe Theater, also on the south bank, announced the showing of a play in the 16th Century.

Battersea Power Station.
Computer axonometric. The computer axonometric drawing approaches the renovated facility through the entrance in the listed wall and cuts away to reveal the stepping floorplates. The red wall is a 100-foot-high kinetic mural, whose changing visual imagery will set the pace for transformation of the space at regular intervals.

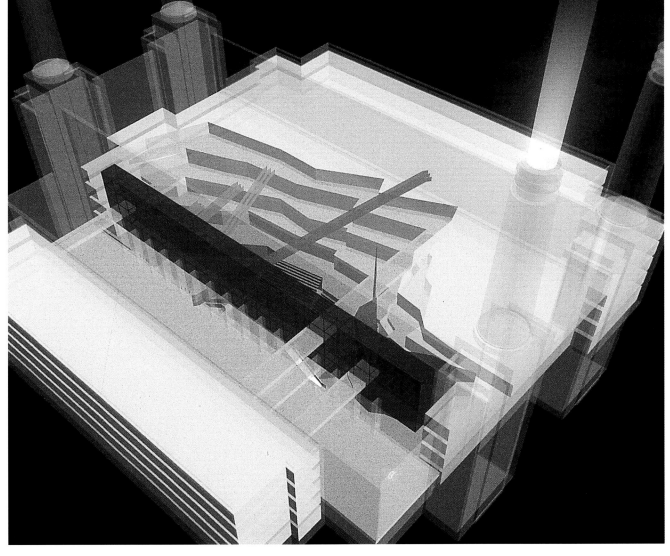

Battersea Power
Station.
The model provides
a view through the
kinetic mural to show
circulation in the main
space of the power
station.

Battersea Power
Station.
Gilbert Gorski's
plaza-level rendering
of a modern "town
square" indicates
the scale of the
proposed Battersea
entertainment complex

and the variety of the
proposed spaces, which
will include sports
attractions, themed
speciality retail,
restaurants, nightclubs,
and a broad variety
of theater and gallery
experiences.

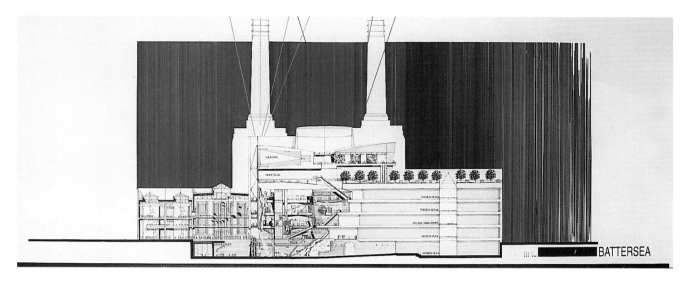

Battersea Power Station.
The section shows the interactive layering of retail pavilions and entry portals with nightclub and theater venues flanking a large indoor/outdoor garden. The Power Station is the centerpiece of a planned multi-million-square-foot development to include office, hotel, and entertainment spaces.

Plus Ultra Discovery Park
Veracruz, Mexico

As Gensler's project for London's Battersea Power Station starts to define the new frontiers of the urban entertainment complex, the expanding notion of entertainment begins to embrace education and vacation as well. There is nothing new about creating architecture around the intersection of vacation and entertainment - just think of Disney World, for example. With Gensler's proposal for Veracruz, Mexico, however, the entertainment offered and the architecture built to sustain it are grounded in notions of local history, culture, and folklore. This plan for the waterfront site calls for the construction of "Pavilions of Discovery" designed to convey authentic history, culture, and science through exhibits and multimedia environments. The plan also incorporates pavilions dedicated to the history of both Mexico and Veracruz as well as an exhibition hall on the overall theme of discovery. An adjacent theme park, which is also included in the overall plan "Legends and Adventures," is planned to be divided into zones based on historic eras that will attempt to illustrate the folk history and popular tales of Veracruz and Mexico. Centrally located among archeological sites representing each era of Mexico's history, the Plus Ultra Discovery Park will act as a research base, learning center, and stepping-off point for further exploration of the region.

Plus Ultra Discovery
Park.
The plan of Plus Ultra
Discovery Park
distinguishes true
history and culture in
the Pavilions of
Discovery at left from
folklore and fantasy in
the theme park at right.
Linking the two is the
food, retail, and live
entertainment center,
Festival Plaza.

Plus Ultra Discovery
Park.
In the theme park
"Legends and
Adventures," zones
based on historic eras
bring the folk history
and popular tales of
Veracruz and Mexico to
life. Shown is Festival
Town, with rides and
shows themed to
traditional village
festivals.

Plus Ultra Discovery
Park.
The Pavilions of
Discovery convey
authentic history,
culture, and science
through exhibits and
multimedia
environments. Pavilions
of Mexico [Left] and
Veracruz [Right] flank
an exhibition hall
dedicated to the overall
theme of discovery.

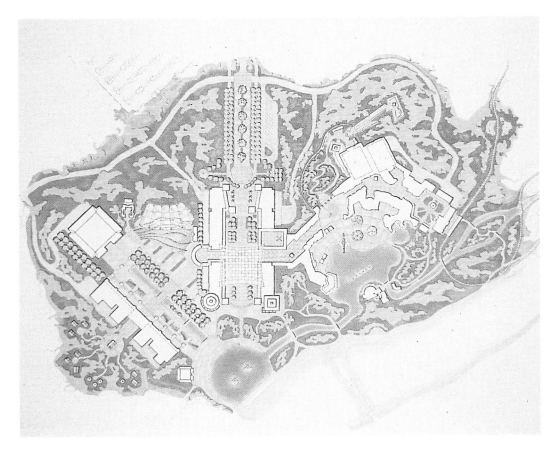

KPIX, Channel 5

Some of the earliest work Gensler did for the communications-technology industry was for KPIX (Channel 5) in San Francisco, California. Gensler was retained in 1978 to orchestrate the transformation of a 220,000-square-foot, five-story structure, originally built in 1909, into an electronic news-gathering and production facility. KPIX required studios and administrative offices that were to occupy only the top two floors of the building. The Gensler team of architects designed the remaining 90,000 square feet of space for multitenant use. In order to accommodate studio production facilities, the Gensler team raised the roof to thirty feet, leaving the exterior of this early concrete structure virtually unchanged. At the ground level, the original loading bays were restructured by the Gensler team to provide the KPIX mobile minicam vans with quick access to the studios within. The Gensler design for the structure also called for the conversion of the original basement into a parking garage for approximately 100 cars.

The Gensler architects and designers wanted to establish and maintain a separate identity for KPIX within the multitenant structure. To do so they designed a separate building entry and elevator lobby for KPIX and renovated the existing entrances for tenant use. The architects located KPIX's administrative offices on the fourth floor and reserved the fifth floor for their technical control center, two major production studios, green rooms, and a scenery shop. The architects then connected these elements with an interior staircase capped by a skylight, which centralized the two floors and provided an autonomous feeling within the multitenant structure.

KFIX.
Plan of the 5th floor
technical facilities.

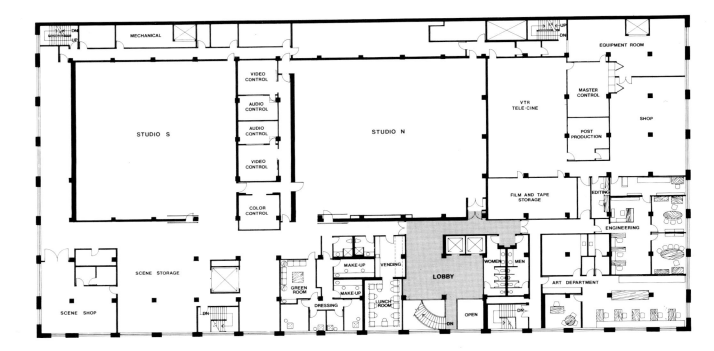

KPIX, Studio.
KPIX interior spaces are
divided between 4th
floor administrative
offices and a 5th floor
technical area, which is
reserved for technical
control center, and two
major production
studios, one of which is
shown below.

At right
KPIX, Exterior.
The Gensler architects
renovated an historic
post-earthquake
building to meet the
specialized electronic
news-gathering and
production needs of
KPIX (Channel 5)
television studios and
administrative offices

and to convert the
balance of space for
tenant use.
One of the earliest
concrete structures in
the north central
waterfront area of San
Francisco, the five-story
building built in 1909,
looks virtually
unchanged on the
exterior. A new glazing

treatment complements
the basic architectural
character, while
portions of the roof
have been raised to
thirty feet to
accommodate studio
production
requirements - an
alteration accomplished
without changing the
building facade.

 ABC/KGO

The American Broadcasting Company's KGO in San Francisco, California, retained the Gensler architects in 1982 to remodel a three-story office and computer facility in order to yield the 168,000 square feet necessary to accommodate offices and broadcast studios for KGO-TV, and KGO-AM and FM radio. The project included major structural alterations in order to create two thirty-two-foot-high television studios designed to be easily adaptable for future changes in the industry and a two-story scene shop and technical area. Depressed slabs were used on some of the flooring to provide later access, and all the floors, walls, and ceilings of the television studios are acoustically separated from the rest of the building by spring isolators. The Gensler team also refitted the entire building with the appropriate heating, ventilation, and air-conditioning systems as well as electrical distribution, cooling towers, and chillers. The team of designers provided the office areas with a simple, modern atmosphere that resounds with efficiency.

ABC/KGO, Reception. The reception features a 1985 streamlined aesthetic, a clean and simple solution incorporating dramatic color combinations and technology.

ABC/KGO, Studio.
The floors, walls and
ceilings of the TV
studios are acoustically
separated from the rest
of the building by
spring isolators.

ABC/KGO, Studio.
The building was
refitted with new,
larger HVAC systems,
electrical distribution,
cooling towers and
chillers. Technical areas
feature depressed slabs
for access flooring.

ABC/KGO, Studio.
Major structural
changes created two
large, 32-foot-high TV
studios designed to be
easily adaptable to
future changes in the
industry.

KQED

Initially KQED had considered renovating their previous location, but after a feasibility study executed by the Gensler team of planners and architects, KQED chose to move to a new location. This decision was based on the cost and the amount of disruption that would be caused by working in a phased construction site for a period of years. An existing 155,000-square-foot, three-story industrial warehouse was chosen. In 1989 the Gensler team started the total redesign of this lofty space to yield the required television and radio studios, along with the necessary administrative and support facilities for this public broadcasting station.

The Gensler team had to consider the limited budget of the public broadcasting organization and simultaneously meet technical broadcasting requirements. Acoustical constraints, for example, demanded strict attention to the design and detailing of all of the building's new mechanical and electrical systems. A sizable portion of the existing post-tensioned concrete floor slabs and columns had to be removed in order to attain the thirty-eight-foot floor-to-ceiling heights required for KQED's largest television studio. With this in mind, the architects placed an atrium, which also serves as a much-needed audience-holding area, adjacent to the studio, by creating one of the largest holes ever cut into a post-tensioned slab. The premium for opening the center of the sprawling building was made even greater by the free-form, curved skylight the architects cut from the roof above. Forty-three windows were also added to the exterior facade to bring in much-needed light.

The atrium became the predominant design feature of the building, providing necessary visual and spatial relief from the expansive, 51,000-square-foot floors. The Gensler team then created a central pedestrian artery from the building entrance towards this central atrium, which is flanked by a slowly curving wall. This warm, ochre-colored wall is perfectly vertical at the entry lobby, but arches radically as it proceeds along the corridor. Eventually it peels back to reveal the thirty-foot-high atrium. Leaning into the atrium as its curve increases, the wall leans into the space by as much as fifteen feet before slicing through the roof to expose the 120-foot-long skylight. The skylight narrows as the atrium funnels back into the entry lobby, where the all-important dynamism of this wall penetrates the front face of the building as well as the roof, to create a forty-foot-high marquee for the station's call letters.

On the upper floor, the Gensler architects created a fifty-four-foot-long pedestrian bridge to span the atrium, providing the staff above with visual access to the activities within the atrium below. As the atrium was designed to become the center of public access within the building, the technical and support areas as well as both television studios were placed nearby along with a boardroom, which was treated so it can double as a radio studio for broadcasts involving large groups.

The Gensler team also designed the building's signs and a system of simple graphic elements that are placed within the floors and on the walls to recognize contributors.

At right
KQED, exterior, main entrance.
The entry is punctuated by a 40-foot-high marquee bearing the company's call letters. This sign marks the end of a curved corridor wall that draws visitors and staff to the new central atrium from the elevator lobby.

KQED, Building
Sections.
Sections through the
proposed building plan
demonstrate the
vertical spatial
relationship of the
atrium with studio,
television offices, and
publishing space, as
well as circulation and
parking functions
within the building.

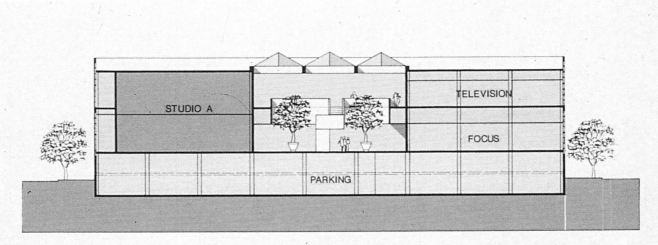

WEST/EAST BUILDING SECTION

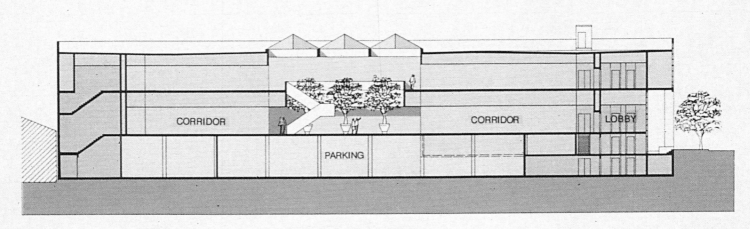

NORTH/SOUTH BUILDING SECTION

KQED, Second-level
Floor Plan.
This preliminary
conceptual design,
which was later altered,
shows the main
technical level, which
would house KQED's
television studios,
control rooms, support
facilities, and offices for
a small publishing
operation.

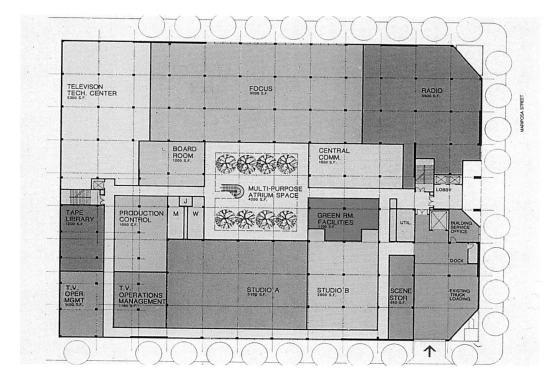

KQED, Third-level Floor
Plan.
This conceptual design,
which was later altered,
shows how a proposed
square central atrium
would relate to
television studios,
administrative space,
and executive offices.

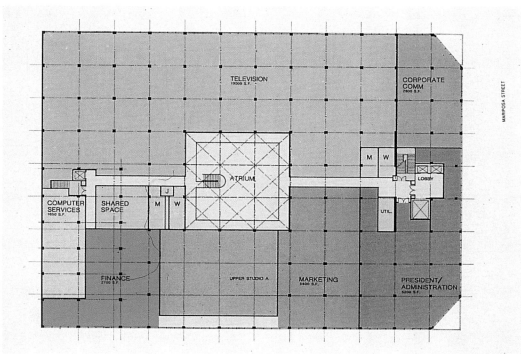

KQED, Parking-level
Floor Plan.
Proposed parking-level
plan demonstrating
large additional parking
spaces adjacent to the
existing parking area.
New storage space is
shown on the right.

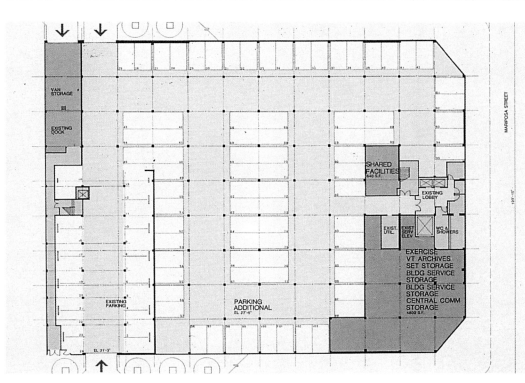

KQED, Exterior. Addition of 43 windows brought much-needed light into the interior of the once dark warehouse and increased the visual appeal of the rather plain exterior.

KQED, floor plan.
The second floor of the
KQED facility houses
their two television
studios, technical
operations, FM radio
facility, and magazine
publishing operations.
The plan view illustrates
how the atrium is a
multi-purpose space
that serves not only for
circulation but also for
audience holding, staff
gatherings, and public
receptions.

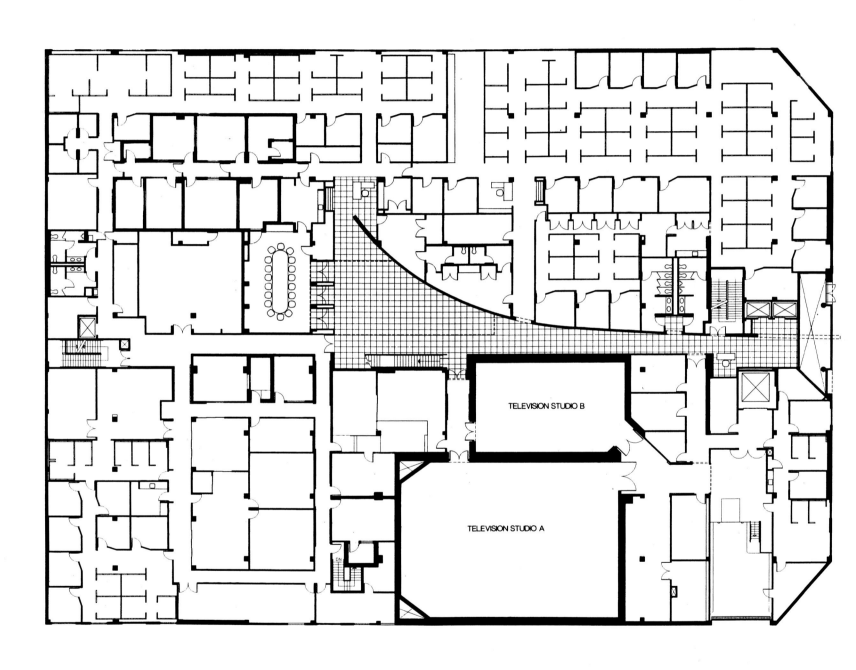

TELEVISION STUDIO B

TELEVISION STUDIO A

KQED, Reception.
The new quarters bring
KQED to a more
advanced stage in its
growth, transforming
the building into a
facility capable of
housing all staff and
technical operations
under one roof in the
most imaginative way.
Clean, simple materials
set against strong
neutral colors on walls
and floors reinforce the
efficient, streamlined
image of a modern
broadcasting station.

KQED, Work-station at
Atrium Bridge.
The expansive office
areas for administration
and support staff are
enhanced with a 13-
foot-high ceiling.
Suspended indirect light
fixtures provide a soft,
even illumination
throughout.

KQED, Seating Area.
The sloped wall creates
unexpected spaces to
sit, an unusual feature
in a dramatically open
space. The wall leans
into this space by as
much as 15 feet and
slices through the roof
to expose a 120-foot-
long skylight. The
skylight narrows as the
atrium funnels back
into the entry lobby,
where the wall
penetrates the front
face of the building as
well as the roof.

KQED, Signage.

KQED, Contribution
Wall.
Along a major wall
contributors are
recognized in simple,
clean graphic elements.

Graphic - KQED, Private
Office.
Signage elements relate
to the elements of the
Contribution Wall.

At right
KQED, Atrium Bridge.
The bold use of color,
geometric architectural
elements, the skylight,
and a 54-foot-long
pedestrian bridge
spanning the space
made the atrium a
point of orientation for
the expansive floors
and a dynamic
environment for staff
meetings and studio
audiences.

KQED, Television
Studio.
The 38-foot floor-to-
floor heights created by
removing a large
portion of the post-
tensioned slab are
ideally suited for the
new television studio.

KQED, Atrium. Working within the constraints of a limited budget, the Gensler team concentrated not on detailing and expensive finishes, but on a strong design concept. This project features one of the largest holes ever cut into a post-tensioned slab, to create a central atrium on the second floor, illuminated by natural light through a free-form curved skylight cut from the roof.

KQED, Atrium Corridor. A central pedestrian artery is flanked by a slowly curving feature wall, which unfolds as a unique surprise for visitors. This warm, butterscotch-colored wall is perfectly vertical at the entry lobby and then arcs ever more radically as it proceeds along the corridor. At the same time, it leans at a steeper angle, eventually peeling away to reveal the 35-foot-high atrium.

Vallejo
Performing Arts
Conference
Center

The Gensler team of planners, architects and designers began working on this multiphased project for the City Council of Vallejo, California, in May of 1994. The first phase of the project included an analysis of a full range of potential sites for this performing arts/conference center. Beyond their architectural and design services, the Gensler team led a fourteen-person committee representing a cross section of interests in Vallejo, including business and arts groups, toward the development of a mission statement, site evaluation criteria, preliminary cost estimates, financial feasibility, and a matrix to compare and rank sites. The work displayed here illustrates concepts for various chosen sites.

Vallejo Performing Arts
Conference Center.
Preliminary concept
drawing for a potential
site.

Vallejo Performing Arts
Conference Center.
Preliminary concept
drawing for a potential
site.

American Conservatory Theater

In 1991, after the eighty-two-year-old Geary Theater was badly damaged by the 1989 earthquake, the American Conservatory Theater retained Gensler to develop a seismically sound environment and overall design concept for the theater and to take the project through the process of reconstruction. The Gensler team incorporated a floor-to-roof shear wall at the rear of the main auditorium to seismically stabilize the building. The location of this wall provided space for several new lobbies, restrooms, and lounge areas at all levels. The reconstruction and seismic upgrade necessitated the reorganization of the theater seating, and although the overall seating capacity will be reduced, the sightlines and comfort have been greatly improved. The Gensler team has incorporated modern theater technology throughout the theater: elevators have been designed to service all floors, and life safety has been improved. The architects have also relocated and upgraded the stage control room, stage lighting and stage floor, and replaced all backstage rigging and dressing rooms. The overall plan calls for the creation of a state-of-the-art, modern theater without destroying the historic warmth and intimacy of the space.

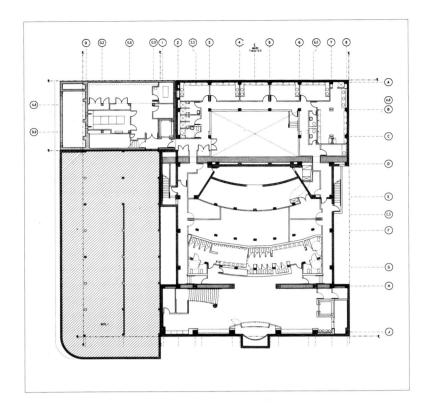

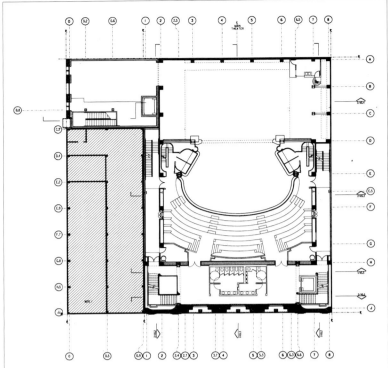

American Conservatory
Theater.
Plan of the lower
lounge level.
This plan of the lower
lounge level shows
lounge, restrooms,
storage and support
spaces, dressing rooms,
and stage pit.

American Conservatory
Theater.
Plan of upper balcony.
The upper balcony plan
depicts the upper
lounge, a totally new
element, the new
technical control booth,
and refurbished seating
area. The Gensler team
also added support
space, such as dressing
rooms and production
offices.

American Conservatory
Theater.
Plan of the balcony
level.
The plan of the balcony

level shows front-of-
house space, lounge,
restrooms, shear wall,
and refurbished seating
area.

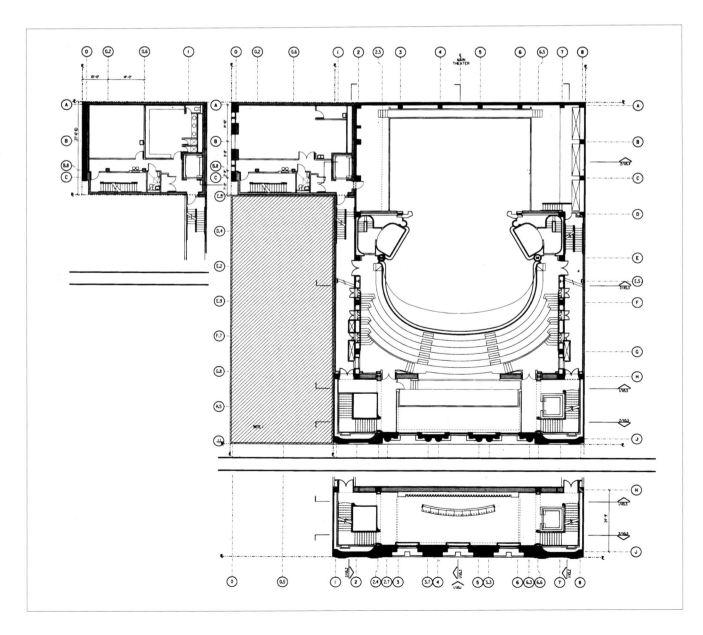

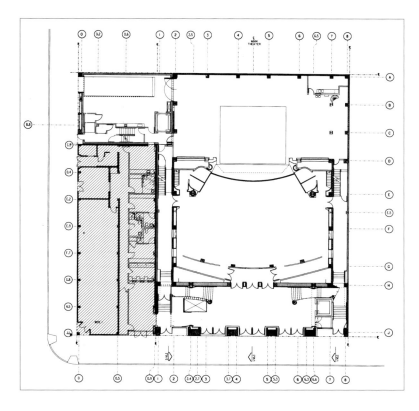

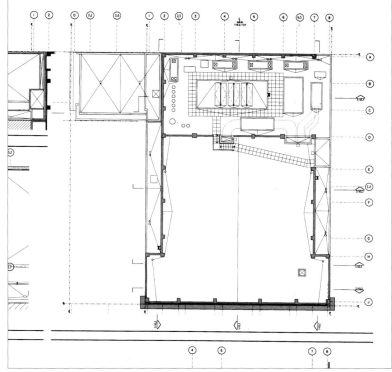

American Conservatory
Theater.
Plan of orchestra level.
The orchestra-level plan
shows the new scenery

storage area in an
annex that was
renovated by Gensler
architects.

American Conservatory
Theater.
Roof plan.

American Conservatory
Theater.
Line drawing of the
historic theater.
This line drawing of the
historic theater closely
resembles the restored
structure.

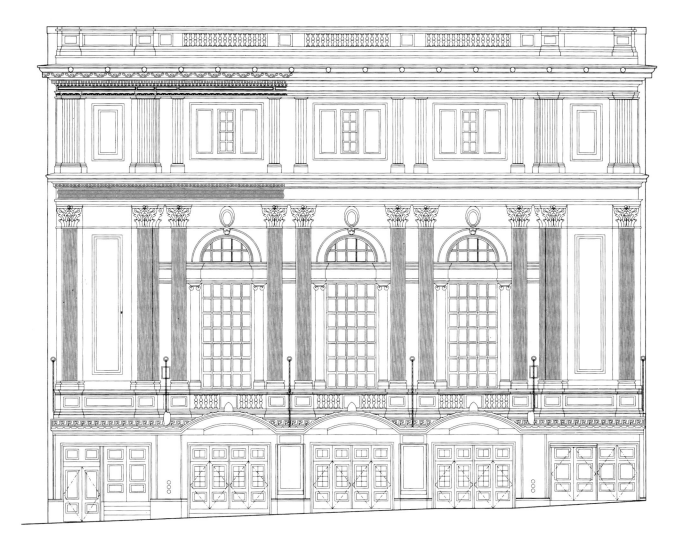

American Conservatory
Theater.
Rendering of the
historic 1909 Geary
Street facade.
This drawing, by
Gensler designer
William Wilde, depicts
the historic 1909 Geary
Street facade.

At right
American Conservatory
Theater.
Stage under
construction as seen
from balcony.
This photograph was
taken from the balcony
level looking at the
stage under
construction. The
grillwork and roof
above stage have been
removed.

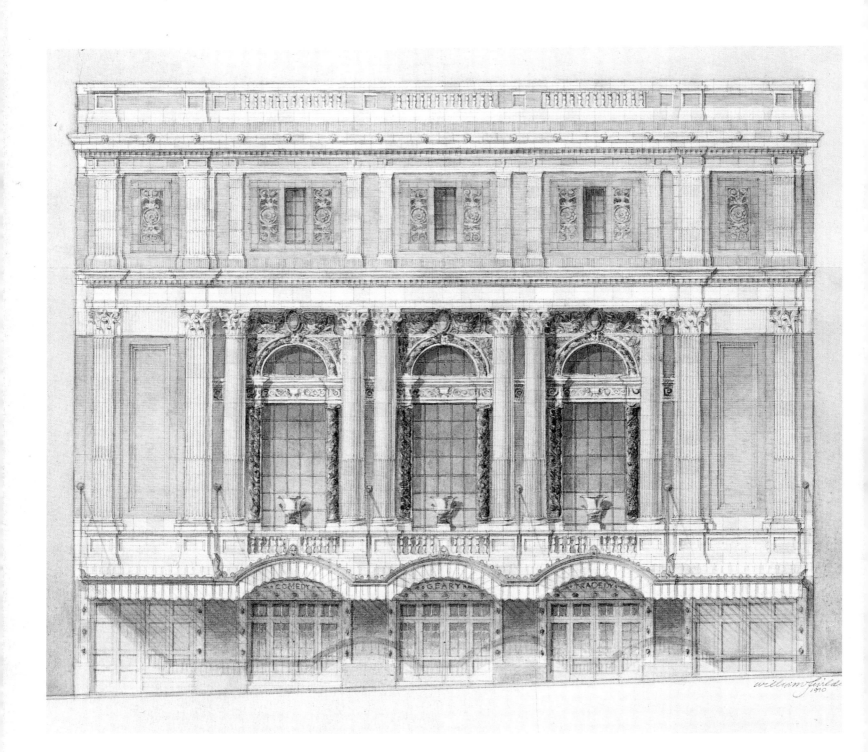

Beverly Hills Hotel

People who love old buildings generally start to shiver when they hear of planned renovations. They immediately think that restoration means the most total devastation a building can endure, and worse, they often picture an ersatz replication of the building that no longer exists. Perhaps this is often the case, but with the restoration and renovation the Gensler team of architects and designers executed for the Beverly Hills Hotel, the scenario is quite a different one. Their absolute presence here goes almost unnoticed. In a *New York Times* article entitled "Real Hollywood Never Died: It was Just Being Renovated," published shortly after completion of the project in the spring of 1995, the writer praises the outcome of the renovation but makes no mention of the painstaking work of the Gensler architects. This is somewhat like publicly complimenting a friend who has just returned from a month's vacation in Switzerland looking twenty years younger by saying, "You look wonderful," while thinking, "Your doctor is a genius" – when the past is improved, it is what existed before that takes the credit.

The challenge for the Gensler architects on this project was to bring the Beverly Hills Hotel up to 1990s speed without destroying what was left of the original 1912 and subsequent 1940s Paul Williams design. The team also had to reinforce the residential imagery of the exterior facades, gardens, and entrances while totally reconstructing and expanding support services, upgrading vehicular circulation, and optimizing revenue potential. The Gensler design reduced the number of rooms but notably raised their quality. The hotel's public spaces were not increased, but the Gensler design has increased their capacity and greatly improved their circulation, support services, and functioning.

The design also significantly reduced noise and vented emissions and created a new three-level subterranean parking garage. The renovation also added a tea lounge, a fine-dining restaurant and a grand stair to the Crystal Ballroom. In the above-mentioned *New York Times* article the hotel's general manager is quoted as saying, "The only thing that has changed is that the roof doesn't leak." This is like your newly face-lifted friend declaring that the Swiss air is responsible for her swift rejuvenation.

The Gensler design for the hotel has restored vitality to all of the guest accommodations, both in the main hotel and in the surrounding cabanas and bungalows. The ballrooms, pre-function areas, famous Polo Lounge, coffee shop, tennis courts, and swimming pool have all been restored, upgraded, and revitalized to meet the fantastic expectations visitors have of the hotel. As with much of Gensler's work with the entertainment industry, the Beverly Hills Hotel needed to inhabit a realm beyond the normal criteria of scale, proportion, comfort, and taste we normally attribute to hotel architecture – the building itself had to be entertaining.

Beverly Hills Hotel, Grand stair.
The most dramatic feature of the entry sequence is Gensler's grand stair which descends from the lobby to the Crystal Ballroom. From the landing, guests have a panoramic view of Sunset Boulevard as it winds westward toward the ocean.

Beverly Hills Hotel, Main lobby.
The circular lobby recaptures the warmth of the original Hotel. It is the center from which all functions radiate.

Beverly Hills Hotel, C Wing.
The original and beloved Paul Williams design from the 1940s is splendidly restored, with the signature Beverly Hills Hotel sign. Set in a lush 12-acre garden, the Beverly Hills Hotel is a unique destination resort.

On the following pages Beverly Hills Hotel, Swimming pool. Though the pool remains exactly as it was before, the historic cabanas have been totally refurbished. At twilight, the new ballroom wing and grand staircase are reflected in the pool.

Since its founding in 1965, Gensler *Architecture, Design and Planning Worldwide* has grown to one of the largest international design firms, with over 800 professionals worldwide. Known as the "Architect of Ideas" for its creative solutions to a continually expanding diversity of design challenges, Gensler maintains a broad-based practice in architecture, interior design, planning services, resource management, and graphic design. The firm has offices in Atlanta, Boston, Denver, Detroit, Hong Kong, Houston, Irvine (CA), London, Los Angeles, New York, Parsippany (NJ), San Francisco, Tokyo, and Washington, DC. In addition to the Gensler entertainment practice, other areas of focus for the firm include office buildings, high-performance work environments, airports, retail and hospitality, as well as strategic facilities planning, facilities management, and Gensler Information Solutions. Gensler holds the unique distinction of having achieved Number One rankings in independent surveys conducted by the following publications: *Interior Design, World Architecture, Facilities Design & Management, Building Design and Construction,* and *Commercial Renovation.* The firm was recognized in 1995 as Firm of the Year by the California Council of the American Institute of Architects and is recipient of an award for excellence in general management from the Professional Services Management Association.

Gensler Teams, Associated Architects, and Consultants

SONY PICTURES STUDIOS
(master plan and various buildings)
Gensler Team:
Principal
Edward Friedrichs
Project Principal
Bruce Campbell
Project Director
T. Michael Darner
Design Director
Robert Green
Project Manager
Anthony Micu
Project Manager
David Fridlund
Project Manager
Leland Karasick
Project Manager
Chris Mehren
Fred Dagdagan
John Scouffas
Bill Fauber
Bill Lim
Bruce Hammer
Catherine Shields
Chari Thralls
Charles Shores
David Takeuchi
Gary Golden
Huston Eubank
Jil Francisco
Joe Verbrugge
John Carter
Judy Amaya
Ken Gilbert
Mark Runge
Mike Kreski
Richard Berliner
Robben Mayer
Steve Adams
Walter Albrecht

Consultants:
Acoustical
Smith Fause & Associates
Audio / Visual
Paul S. Veneklasen & Associates
Civil
Rogoway / Borkovetz Associates
Psomas & Assoc.
Food Service
Cini-Little International
General Contractor
Swinerton & Walberg Company
Landscape
Larry Moline Ltd.

Lighting
Joe Kaplan Architectural Lighting

Project Management
Stegeman and Kastner, Inc.
Structural Engineer
Entertainment Engineering, Inc.
MEP
Levine / Seegel & Assoc.

Photography
Marco Lorenzetti / Hedrich Blessing

WARNER BROS.
Triangle Building
Gensler Team:
Principal
Edward Friedrichs
Project Manager
Scott Kaufman
Project Architect
Richard Berliner
Project Designer
Lee Pasteris
Catherine Shields
Diane Stoll

Consultants:
Civil
Rogoway / Borkovetz Associates
General Contractor
Peck/Jones Construction Corp.
Landscape
The SWA Group
Lighting
PHA Lighting Design
Security
API Security, Inc.
Structural Engineer
Ove Arup & Partners
Vertical Transportation
John Hess & Associates
MEP
Ove Arup & Partners

Photography
Paul Bielenberg
Erhard Pfeiffer

Columbia Pictures and the Lady and Torch design are trademarks of Columbia Pictures Industries Inc.

TriStar Pictures and the Pegasus design are trademarks of TriStar Pictures Inc.

WARNER BROS.
Pavilion
Gensler Team:
Principal
Marvin Taff
Project Manager / Architecture

Frederick Dagdagan
Designer / Interiors
Lee Pasteris
Designer / Architecture
James Hall
Associated Arch:
Kaplan / McLaughlin / Diaz

Consultants:
Acoustical
Charles M. Salter & Associates
Civil
Tate Associates
Cost
Adamson Associates
General Contractor
Turner Construction Company
Landscape
Emmet L. Wemple & Associates
Lighting
S.L. Auerbach and Associates
Structural Engineer
KPFF Consulting Engineers
MEP
Rosenberg & Associates

Photography
Erhard Pfeiffer

WARNER BROS.
Feature Production Building
Gensler Team:
Principal
Edward Friedrichs
Project Principal
Deborah Baron
Project Manager / Architecture
Scott Kaufman
Project Manager / Interiors
Ruth Gilliland
Project Architect
Richard Berliner
Architect
Stuart Stephens
Project Designer
Lee Pasteris
Technical Support
Keith Kaneko

Consultants:
General Contractor
Turner Construction Company
Landscape
Emmet L. Wemple & Associates
Lighting
Joe Kaplan Architectural Lighting
Structural Engineer
Brandow & Johnston Associates
MEP
Syska & Hennessy, Inc.

Photography
Nick Merrick / Hedrich Blessing

WARNER BROS.
Main Administration Building
Gensler Team:
Project Principal
Deborah Baron
Project Manager
Ruth Gilliland
Project Designer
Lee Pasteris
John Fugle
Chris Mehren

Consultants:
Civil
Psomas & Associates
Fire/Life Safety
API Security, Inc.
General Contractor
Turner Construction Company
Geotechnical
Law-Crandell, Inc.
Landscape
Emmet L. Wemple & Associates
Lighting
Horton-Lees Lighting Design, Inc.
Security
API Security, Inc.
Structural Engineer
KPFF Consulting Engineers
Traffic/Transportation
Crain & Associates
MEP
Syska & Hennessy, Inc.

Photography
Nick Merrick / Hedrich Blessing

WARNER BROS.
Commissary
Gensler Team:
Project Principal
Deborah Baron
Project Manager / Architect
Ruth Gilliland
Project Designer
Lee Pasteris
Lorraine Francis
Keith Kaneko

Consultants:
General Contractor
Turner Construction Company
Lighting
Joe Kaplan Architectural Lighting
Structural Engineer

Brandow & Johnston Associates
MEP
Syska & Hennessy, Inc.

Photography
Nick Merrick / Hedrich Blessing

WARNER BROS.
Master Plan
Gensler Team:
Director
Marty Borko
Alireza Badie
Nancy Coleman-Romanos
David DeSelm
Fred Dagdagan
Mike Kreski

Consultants:
Civil
Psomas & Associates
Geotechnical
Kovacs-Byer & Associates
Traffic/Transportation
Crain & Associates

Photography
copyrighted by Warner Bros., Inc.

PARAMOUNT PICTURES
Master Plan / Melrose Office Building /
Paramount Theater
Gensler Team:
Principal
Edward Friedrichs
Director
Andrew Cohen
Project Architect, Master Plan
Eugene Watanabe
Project Architect, Theatre
Stuart Stephens
Project Architect, Office Building
Ron Takaki
Project Designer
Barbara Dunn
Project Programmer
Anne Ferree
Project Manager
Anna Marie Howell
Steven Adams
Jeff Hall
Susan Orlandi

Consultants:
Acoustical
Charles M. Salter Associates, Inc.
Communications
Hutton Graber & Associates

Civil
Jack K. Bryant & Associates, Inc.
Environmental
Environmental Science Associates, Inc.
General Contractor
Peck/Jones Construction Corp.
Landscape
Emmett L. Wemple & Associates
Legal
Manatt, Phelps, Rothberg & Phillips
Lighting
Wheel Gertzkoff Friedman & Shankar
Structural Engineer
Brandow & Johnston Associates
Traffic / Transportation
Crain & Associates
Vertical Transportation
Lerch, Bates & Associates
MEP
Syska & Hennessy, Inc.

Photography
Marco Lorenzetti / Hedrich Blessing

PARAMOUNT PICTURES
Commissary
Gensler Team:
Principal
Edward Friedrichs
Project Interior Designer
Phyllis Farrell
Project Designer
Tim Clement
Imre Takacs

Consultants:
Electrical Engineer
Nikolas Patsaouras & Associates, Inc.
Food Service
Laschober & Sovich, Inc.
General Contractor
C.W. Driver, Inc.
Millwork
C.W. Driver, Inc.
MEP.
Syska & Hennessy, Inc.

Photography
Jaime Ardiles-Arce

BABELSBERG STUDIOS
Gensler Team:
Principal
Edward Friedrichs
Design Principal
Andrew Cohen
Director / Project Manager
T. Michael Darner

Designer
James Hall
Architect / Designer
Gerhard Mayer
Architect
Huston Eubank
Designer
Robben Mayer

Associated Arch:
Valode & Pistre et Associes

Architects of Record:
Bayerer Hanson Heidenreich Schuster
Krause & Cardillo

Consultants:
Structural Engineer
Weiske-Partner
Engineer
Ingeniere Sechaude & Bossuyt
Studio Hamburg
Legal
Beiten Burkhardt Mittl & Wegener
Computer
Cologne Media Lab

STUDIO PLAZA
Gensler Team:
Principal
Edward Friedrichs
Project Principal
Bruce Campbell
Project Manager
T. Michael Darner
Project Manager
Theodora Huddleston
Project Designer
Robert Green
Project Designer
Marvin Taff
Douglas Bregenzer
Lamar Johnson
Keith Kaneko
Alberto Lima
Lee Pasteris
Reynaldo Osegueda
John Thiele
Kris Walsh
Steven Weinstein
Nora Wolin
Shahrzad Zamanpour
James McNett
Gabriel Armendariz

Consultants:
Landscape
P.O.D.

Structural Engineer
John A. Martin Associates
Mechanical/Electrical
Levine / Seegel & Associates
General Contractor
Peck / Jones Construction Corp.
Project Management
Stegeman and Kastner
Lighting
Patrick Quigley Assoc. / Jules Horton
Acoustics
Paul S. Veneklasen Associates
Furniture Dealer
CRI

Photography
Erhard Pfeiffer
Stanley Klimek
Jon Miller / Hedrich Blessing
Marco Lorenzetti / Hedrich Blessing

SONY THEATRES, LINCOLN SQUARE
Gensler Team:
Project Director
T. Michael Darner
Design Director
Robert Green
Project Manager
David Fridlund
Charles Shores, Jr.
Steven Weinstein
Claus Best
Daniel Jansenson
John Scouffas
Huston Eubank
Ruth Laug
Steven Adams
Richard Hansen
Douglas Bregenzer

Arch. of Record
Schuman, Lichtenstein, Claman,
Effron Architects

Base Building Architect
Kohn Pedersen Fox Associates

Consultants:
Acoustical
Shen Milsom & Wilke, Inc.
Construction Management
Lehrer McGovern Bovis, Inc.
Cost
Rider Hunt Levett & Carey, Ltd.
General Contractor
Lehrer McGovern Bovis, Inc.
Lighting
Gallegos Lighting Design

Structural Engineer
Robert Rosenwasser Associates
Mech./Elec.
James Cooper Associates

Photography
Marco Lorenzetti / Hedrich Blessing
Andrew Bordwin

BATTERSEA POWER STATION
Gensler Team:
Principal
Edward Friedrichs
Architecture Principal
Andrew Cohen
Design Principal
T. Michael Darner
Peter Ullathorne
Alan Grant
Randy Guillot
Jeff Hall
Tetsuya Ogami
Craig Shimahara
Mike Kreski

Associated Architect
RHWL (Renton Howard Wood Leven)
/ London
Geoffrey Mann

Consultants:
Economic Research Associates
John Robinett

Owner:
Parkview International Ltd.
Victor Hwang
Michael Roberts
Charles Madden

Developer
The Gordon Company
Sheldon Gordon, President

PLUS ULTRA DISCOVERY PARK
Gensler Team:
Concept Development
Thomas Ito
Marty Borko
Michael Kreski

Consultants:
Economics / Market Analysis
Economic Research Associates
Program Development
Strategic Leisure, Inc.

KPIX
Gensler Team:

Principal
Charles Kridler
Designer
Louise A. Elmquist
Project Arcitect
Clonia Cautis

Consultants:
Acoustical
Robert A. Hansen Associates, Inc.
Civil
Martin M. Ron Associates
General Contractor
Dinwiddie Construction Corp.
Structural Engineer
Peter Culley & Associates
Mech./Elec.
Syska & Hennessy, Inc.

Photography
Paul Bielenberg

AMERICAN BROADCASTING COMPANIES (ABC) / KGO
Gensler Team:
Principal
Charles Kridler
Alphonse T. Allison

Photography
Mark Citret

KQED
Gensler Team:
Principal
Charles Kridler
Design Director
Robert Wheatley
Project Manager
Kevin Schaeffer
Designer
John Scouffas
Designer / Interiors
Debra Cibilich
Designer / Interiors
Mimi Chin
Programmer
Frederick Yasaki
Graphic Design Director
John Bricker
Graphic Designer
Thomas Horton

Consultants:
Acoustical
Charles M. Salter & Associates
Broadcast / Technical
National Teleconsultants, Inc.

General Contractor
Cahill Contractors, Inc.
Structural Engineer
Steven Tipping & Associates
MEP.
Syska & Hennessy, Inc.

Photography
Chas McGrath

VALLEJO PERFORMING ARTS/CONFERENCE CENTER
Gensler Team:
Principal
Peter Gordon
Project Manager
Cory Creath
Designer / Architecture
Kevin Hart
Associated Architects:
Michael Willis & Associates

Consultants:
Cultural Planning
Helene Fried & Associates
Theater & Lighting Design
Auerbach & Associates

AMERICAN CONSERVATORY THEATER
Gensler Team:
Principal
M. Arthur Gensler Jr.
Director
Charles Kridler
Design Director
Robert Wheatley
Project Manager / Architect
R.K. Stewart
Designer / Architecture
Bryan Shiles
Designer / Interiors
Debra Cibilich
Luke Sheridan
Kelly Griffin
J.R. Jones
Sherman Takata
Michele Sheehan
Cory Creath
Tom Horton
Kathleen Leonard

Base Building Architect
Bliss & Faville

Consultants:
Audio / Visual
Paoletti Associates, Inc.
Elec.Engineer

Cammisa & Wipf
General Contractor
Cahill Contractors, Inc.
Mechanical Engineer
Guttman & MacRitchie
Structural Engineer
SOH & Associates
Lighting
Auerbach-Glasow
Specification Writer
John Raeber

Photography
Sherman Takata/Gensler

BEVERLY HILLS HOTEL
Gensler Team:
Principal
Edward Friedrichs
Principal
Marvin Taff
Design Director
Andrew Cohen
Project Director, Hotel
Thomas Ito
Project Manager, Bungalows
Anna Marie Howell
Project Manager, Hotel
Caryl Thornton Sherpa
Graphic Design Director
John Bricker
Project Architect
Imre Takacs
Walter Albrecht
Brian Bartholomew
Mike Frey
Cherise Harrington
Keith Kaneko
Alberto Lima
Donna Masada
Robben Mayer
Craig McMahon
Dale Noriyuki
Shirley Spinelli
Alex Yamada

Owner
Sajahtera, Inc.
Manager
Kerman Beriker

Consultants:
Acoustical
Paul S. Veneklasen & Associates
Civil
Psomas and Associates
Environmental
Environmental Science Associates, Inc.

Food Service/ Laundry
Cini-Little International
General Contractor
Peck/Jones Obayashi BHH
Hardware
Finish Hardware Technology
Historic
Mellon & Associates
Interiors
Hirsch Bedner Associates
Landscape
The SWA Group
Lighting
Wheel Gersztoff Friedman Shankar, Inc.
Legal
Erwin, Cohen, Jessup
Project Management
HCB Contractors
Purchasing
Leonard Parker Company
Roofing/Waterproofing
Independent Roofing Consultants
Security
Paul Alan Magil & Associates
Soils
Law/Crandall, Inc.
Structural Engineer
John A. Martin Associates
Telecommunications
Comsul, Ltd.
Traffic/Transportation
Kaku Associates, Inc.
Vertical Transportation
Lerch, Bates & Associates
MEP
Syska & Hennessy,Inc.

Photography
Fred Licht
Erhard Pfeiffer